VIDEO TESTIMONIALS THAT LAND THE BIG FISH

The Proven Marketing Strategy to Attract Bigger Clients, Increase Sales, and Achieve Real YouTube Results with Video Case Stories

IAN GARLIC

Performance Publishing Group
McKinney, TX

ISBN: Paperback 978-1-961781-37-5
ISBN: Hardcover 978-1-961781-07-8
ISBN: Ebook 978-1-961781-98-6

PERFORMANCE
PUBLISHING

CONTENTS

HOW TO USE THIS BOOK

This book is not meant to be read and forgotten. Instead, I encourage you to use it as a reference guide throughout your journey to transform your marketing efforts. Here's a suggested approach:

1. Read the book from cover to cover. Start by absorbing the invaluable insights, strategies, and techniques that I've shared. Gain a deep understanding of the Video Case Story framework and its potential impact on your business.

2. Scan QR Codes (or click links). After you read each chapter, scan the QR codes for supplemental information.

3. Access the toolkit. Visit www.Testimonialbook.com/toolkit.com and explore the wealth of resources available to you. From customizable templates to checklists that ensure no crucial step is overlooked, this toolkit will become your indispensable companion.

4. Don't be afraid to ask for help. You can comment on YouTube videos or email us once you sign up for the Toolkit. You might want some (or all) of this done for you. Go to https://www.videocasestory.com/GetStarted if you have an immediate need for Video Case Stories. You'll connect with a Video Case Story strategist.

5. Commit to action. You'll learn the best way to do that in Chapters 4-6. Come back to each chapter at each phase in your Video Case Story journey.

INTRODUCTION

I was going to start this book with a story about how I first came up with the idea for our video agency. YouTube was purchased by Google in 2007, and online video became easier. Discovering the video you needed through search was now a thing. I realized that attorneys I was working with at the time needed to tell their stories to separate themselves from all the bland marketing that unfortunately still exists in every realm, not just in the legal field.

My father died in 1994. I have many fond memories of my father's entrepreneurial journey before that. We experienced the highs and lows together, from living in a mansion to a tiny apartment with barely enough money for food, and then back to wealth and, ultimately, poverty again before he passed away.

One aspect of my father's life that I didn't have many stories about was his time as a Cadillac salesman. He was the number one salesman in the Midwest. I always thought it was through brute sales force. He was an Underwater Demolitions Expert in the Marines prior to that. The Frogman was the Marine version of the Navy Seal.

Yeah, he was a force.

While editing this book, something happened that profoundly shaped my understanding of the power of customer stories. I interviewed my cousin, Camille, about her memories of my father. She shared fascinating insights about my father's achievements. Camille was like his little sister, a former nun and a high school principal. A whole book can be written on her too. My father was not only the number one Cadillac salesman in the Midwest. He did something that most people still don't do today—he meticulously took notes about his clients. We now have advanced electronic systems for such tasks, but back then, my father manually wrote down on cards every detail about his customers.

He listened attentively to their stories, noting down more than just their names, addresses, and birthdays. He knew their life stories. He knew their kids' birthdays, information about their spouses, and even their anniversaries. He required prospective clients to delay their meeting by at least 30 minutes so he could thoroughly study and understand them. This dedication to understanding his clients inside out, combined with his storytelling skills, set him apart as a salesperson.

That wasn't the last of his accomplishments, by far. The list seems kind of made up.

After leaving Cadillac, my father

- Made the gyro famous in the USA (We're not Greek.)
- Founded JJ Garlics, which at the time was the most famous restaurant in Milwaukee
- Converted a public bathhouse into a restaurant with live dolphin shows, The Public Natatorium
- Lost everything; again moved to Florida
- Sold millions in real Estate in Florida, foretelling the migration to the state

I remember moments of sitting around the table, hearing my father regale us with captivating stories. I witnessed firsthand the power of storytelling, marketing, and building deep connections with customers. It's now evident that three things were the driving force behind his success: his obsession with customer stories, his remarkable marketing/storytelling skills, and his absolute commitment. His achievements, despite his life's various ups and downs, inspired me to continue his legacy.

They say success leaves clues, providing a direct path to achieving greatness.

My marketing obsession may have been the result of my genetic makeup or my upbringing immersed in storytelling. I confidently affirm that being a great storyteller with a focus on customer stories still holds tremendous power today.

The opportunities with Video Case Stories are boundless. Over the past 15 years, I have developed a system to harness their full potential. Building on my father's teachings and my extensive study of success over the past two decades, I'm thrilled to share this transformative knowledge with you.

Before we embark on this journey together, let me leave you with a powerful piece of wisdom my father shared with me.

Whenever I felt stuck or uncertain, he would say,

"Action begets action."

This simple yet profound advice has guided me throughout my life. It is through taking action that we propel ourselves forward and create the future we desire.

Now, let's dive into the realm of Video Case Stories, where we will uncover the secrets to ignite your sales, drive massive traffic, and make you fall in love with your business all over again.

Introduction
Link: https://linke.to/4XoHAL

This book is filled with additional links and QR codes.

Let me explain how to make the most of these valuable resources:

1. QR Codes: As you read each chapter, you'll come across QR codes placed strategically throughout the book. Simply use your smartphone or tablet's camera to scan the QR codes, and you'll be directed to exclusive videos that provide real-life demonstrations, in-depth insights, and additional tips. These videos will enrich your learning experience and take you beyond the written word.
2. www.Testimonialbook.com/toolkit.com: This link grants you access to an exclusive toolkit that complements the concepts explored in the book. Inside, you'll discover valuable templates, checklists, and resources that will streamline your Video Case Story process. Whether you're just getting started or you're a seasoned pro, this toolkit is designed to help you excel in creating captivating customer stories.

HOW TO USE THIS BOOK

This book is not meant to be read and forgotten. Instead, I encourage you to use it as a reference guide throughout your journey in transforming your marketing efforts. Here's a suggested approach:

1. Read the book from cover to cover: Start by absorbing the invaluable insights, strategies, and techniques that I've shared. Gain a deep understanding of the Video Case Story framework and its potential impact on your business.
2. Scan QR Codes (Or Click Links): After you read each chapter, scan the QR codes or click links for supplemental information.
3. Access the toolkit: Visit www.Testimonialbook.com/toolkit.com and explore the wealth of resources available to you. From customizable templates to checklists that ensure no crucial step is overlooked, this toolkit will become your indispensable companion.
4. Don't be afraid to ask for help: You can comment on YouTube videos or email us once you sign up for the Toolkit.

You might want some (or all) of this done for you. Go to VideoCaseStory.com/GetStarted if you have an immediate need for Video Case Stories. You'll get connected with a Video Case Story strategist perfect for your business.

5. Commit to action. You'll learn the best way to do that in Chapter 4.
6. Comeback to each chapter at each phase in your Video Case Story journey

1.0 OVERCOMING THE LIE OF TESTIMONIALS

Of all the liars among mankind, the fisherman is the most trustworthy.
~ William Sherwood Fox

Your customer stories can attract, engage, and "land" the Big Fish—the major clients willing to pay top dollar to work with you. I know because I've been using them to do just that for me and for others for over 17 years, but I must say I did lie.

I said "customer stories," NOT "testimonials." I doubt you've read a book that starts out telling you that the author lied to you. It's just a little lie that happens to be in the title. I guess it's the fisherman in me.

Testimonials will not land the Big Fish.

I used that term because of the big lie most businesses and marketers tell themselves.

"We need testimonials."

You don't. Testimonials are actually hurting your business. This is especially true if your customer value is over $3,000. Testimonials are especially hurting you if you have a customer value of 10, 20, 30, a hundred thousand dollars. You need stories, not testimonials. Specifically, Video Case Stories.

You know what? If you feel deceived, I'm sorry. The great part of this is that Amazon will let you return this book right now for all your money back.

There are so many marketers out there that say you need testimonials.

They will send out a videographer, ask your clients to talk about how great you are, and say, "Here's a testimonial."

You won't know any better.

You might be doing one worse. You just send a list of questions and ask your clients to record their answers on their own.

That does almost nothing to help your business. These testimonials are actually holding your business back.

You're not getting any customer stories. You're not getting any data. You are not getting any emotion.

You're missing opportunities to dig deep and really find the emotions of your customers that drive them in their decision making.

They'll just talk about you. That may feel great, but . . .

New website visitors, new visitors to your YouTube channel, people perusing your LinkedIn don't want to hear about you.

It may hurt, but none of these people care about you.

They only care about what you can do for them.

They care that you've helped someone like them with a problem like theirs achieve the goals that they want.

Your prospects want to see stories like theirs.

Every business needs Video Case Stories. Video Case Stories will transform every marketing campaign. They'll improve your services, your products, and your operation. Video Case Stories will make you happier. I can't overestimate the power of the Video Case story system.

Video Case Stories will help to create amazing offers. Recently, I used it to create a revolutionary offering for one of our clients.

Some of my clients will remain anonymous in this book because I don't want to give away their secrets.

And every single day that we do these Video Case Stories, the system laid out here improves the businesses that are using it.

Don't let the brevity of this book or the simplicity of the system belie their power. I have put years into this. And that's why I'm writing the short version of this book. I want you to use Video Case Stories in the next 90 days.

You can get started sooner. Even if you want to hire one of our Video Case Stories certified strategists, you'll want to take time to listen to this book. This book is not just about promoting our service. It is a step-by-step guide.

It will expedite landing the Big Fish now and for a long time after. The longevity of a great CASE STORY is incredible. Spending a few hours in advance will save you heartache and yield much larger returns.

Some of the Video Case Stories we have created are still in use ten years later, still generating business for our clients. The process works at every point in landing the "Big Fish."

The system I'm going to describe to you here will:

- Generate more highly qualified leads
- Close 32% or more proposals
- Improve rankings in the two biggest search engines
- Help to hire, train, and empower better salespeople
- Create irresistible standout positioning support for your business
- Augment your value propositions
- Massively improve your website performance
- Retain top talent in your business

The Video Case Story system makes your social media just more social. We have used these Video Case Stories in over 50 ways. We are always adding and improving. You can get the latest list in the www.Testimonialbook.com/toolkit.com.

I'm not making this book to just give you tactics. I'm writing this book to transform businesses and lives. I want to empower you to evolve your business, your marketing, and the world. That is not an exaggeration. Video case stories will do just that.

I want you to feel the power that comes with these stories and this system, and the best way to do that is to get you to take action. For that reason, I made this book short, sweet, and to the point. I've never gone through a Video Case Story process completely and thoroughly and not improved a business. I don't want you to have to read 250 pages or listen to 12 hours of an audiobook to implement these systems and strategies.

The marketing campaign you love that brings in the business you want is waiting for you.

The business you love is waiting for you.

Your prospects are waiting for you. Video case stories are the key.

I've produced over 20,000 videos across all industries. Of course, I didn't make them all myself. I had teams. Every single video I've created would have been improved and now is improved through this process.

The teams I've worked with built business websites and executed YouTube and (Search Engine Optimization) for solopreneurs and Fortune 50 companies, as well as large nonprofits, lawyers, doctors, dentists, and other marketing agencies.

Working with other marketing agencies is one thing I'm most proud of. The greatest marketers in the world come to us for their Video Case Stories.

It's like being the doctor's doctor or the lawyer's lawyer.

I've run Facebook ads, YouTube ads, LinkedIn ads, and email campaigns. I've hosted over 400 episodes of the *Garlic Marketing Show* with some of the best business minds and marketers in the world. I've spent hundreds of thousands of dollars on masterminds, courses, workshops, mentors, and coaches.

All these ideas, insights, and experiences are distilled into this book. I can confidently tell you that what you are about to learn will improve everything else you do in marketing and your business.

This is not hyperbole. I've seen almost every business problem in some way, shape, or form solved by this method. In the end, your customer stories are what your business is all about, and video is one of the best ways to tell them.

We have the tools and resources to deliver the Right Story at the Right Time.

If your problem is low profits, low sales, products that clients don't get, or complex services, all of that can be solved with Video Case Stories.

You will begin to win even before your first Case Story interview. Recently, in a Case Story Tackle Box session, the strategy you'll learn in this book, we created a positioning statement that will DOUBLE my client's profits.

Feel like you're lost in the competition? Video case stories are the answer.

Feel like you can't charge enough or attract those bigger clients? We'll solve that here.

Having trouble explaining how you are different from the rest of your industry? Video Case Stories, once again, will fix that.

Is there a lot of complexity to your offering, making it hard to understand? I think you know the answer to that one.

The reason you came here is so that you can start landing those Big Fish—those big clients with high lifetime customer value who love to work with you. You're going to attract them and land them much more easily.

If Video Case Stories were your only strategy, you would still land those Big Fish.

I've done it for myself. You literally could have just a website of amazing Video Case Stories and crush your competition.

Side note: Most websites are watered down "corporate speak." Don't worry. We have a fix for that.

Asking for testimonials and making testimonials will not solve any of your problems. Testimonials cost you massive opportunities. The word alone prevents you from capturing amazing stories.

Great stories transform small businesses. Stories also sit at the Core of the world's most legendary businesses. So, let's start with a quick story about one business and its trash problem.

Scan here for bonus videos on this chapter.

linke.to/VOG6u9

2.0 WHERE ARE THEY GOING TO PUT THEIR HOTDOG WRAPPER?

There was a man who owned a business.

It was a new kind of business. One that had never been seen before. That man, although ultra-wealthy and with thousands of employees, would sit in the window of the entrance of the business and stare at his customers.

He watched them intently.

This man watched how his customers moved through his business. He wasn't watching his customers for theft. This man wasn't counting the number of people coming through the door. He wasn't counting the money he was making. In fact, he really didn't care so much about the money.

This man was actually counting the number of steps his customers took.

He watched when someone bought a hotdog. He wanted to know how far they walked before they threw away the wrapper. It was 30 paces.

That man proceeded to place a trashcan every 30 paces. That man was Walter Elias Disney, and his business, of course, was Disneyland. He insisted everyone call him Walt.

Walt transformed movies and media, and he created the theme park. Walt was an amazing man, an amazing inventor, and an incredible innovator. And he was one of the absolute best storytellers and salesmen of all time. He always could land the Big Fish because he had to. He had to raise money for his movies.

He had to raise a lot of money for Disneyland. Walt put everything on the line. He had to inspire thousands of team members to work for him, sometimes without a paycheck. So, Walt took the information that he learned and not only put a trashcan every 30 steps. He designed a trashcan with a flap on it to prevent flies and to prevent people from seeing the trash every 30 steps. You can go count the steps. I did it the other day.

Trash might not seem like a big deal, but having a clean theme park was. Back then, amusement parks were dirty. He knew how important it was to the people who visited his theme park and how important it was to contribute to being the happiest place on earth. Walt would never have made those changes or invented that trash can had he just sent out a poll to his customers.

He would never have learned that simply by asking his customers to fill out a form at the end of their visit to Disneyland. Visitors will talk about the rides. They talk about the food, but no one mentions the trash cans. But they are a critical part of everyone's enjoyment. Walt could have just worried about how fun the rides were and just sent surveys about that, but he didn't. He knew he needed to make it an amazing experience, and he knew he had to listen to his customers. Truly. Listen.

Walt did something he called "plussing." He wanted to constantly improve every single thing they did at Disneyland, Disney World, in his movies, in his animation, in every way you experience the Walt Disney Company.

Walt's dedication to listening and watching his customers was the key to his growth. That's what truly made Disney, Disneyland, and everything he did great today. The Disney empire is built on those stories. Other stories it is built on are the stories that emerge from the experiences.

The stories of people taking their kids to the park for the first time.

The stories of people getting married at the parks.

The stories of the first time you saw those movies.

Those are the case stories that built the Disney empire.

There's a quote on branding I love. "Branding is something you do to cows. It makes sense if you're a rancher since cows tend to look alike. Branding is what you do when there's nothing original about your product."

That was a quote from Roy Disney, Jr. I'm not saying branding is something we don't need to do. Yes, you should pay attention to your branding, but people buy stories. What makes great brands are the stories behind those brands, and it wasn't just Walt who knew that. Look at the titans that created modern America, the world that we live in today: Ben Franklin, Thomas Edison, Steve Jobs. If not for them, you might not be reading this book. You definitely would not be listening to my podcast. You're probably reading this on a device that's either related to or is directly designed by Steve Jobs, Ben Franklin, or Thomas Edison. They created the future.

The number one talent of all these people was storytelling.

These giants proved the best storyteller always wins. This book about Video Case Stories will set you on the way to being the best storyteller.

Scan here for bonus videos on this chapter.

linke.to/3eQWt6

3.0 THE SWISS ARMY BULLET

As a young boy, I loved Swiss Army Knives. I think I always had a Christmas story-esque vision of being stranded on a mountain.

I don't know how I got to that fantasy mountain.

I was with a group of people—my family and strangers. Everyone was desperate. And then I pulled out my Swiss Army Knife and built a village. I mended everyone's clothes, opened all the bottles, and saved the day. That fantasy probably led me to Video Case Stories.

I've yet to figure out a place in business where Video Case Stories can't be used. We all look for a silver bullet to our problems. It's not a silver bullet. There's never really a silver bullet. Video case stories are not silver bullets. It's a process.

It's more like that Swiss Army Knife that you're going to use to fix things here or there, to improve, and to get things started. The process and outcomes are the closest things I have found to that silver bullet. Video case stories are kind of like a Swiss Army silver bullet. (Great. Now I have to buy another domain.)

Let's dive deeper into some of the ways that you can use Video Case Stories for landing the Big Fish and more.

Video case stories and improving sales

My first Video Case Stories improved my sales. I started using the first version of Video Case Stories in consulting sales in 2007. I was an SEO (Search Engine Optimization) consultant selling my services for a large Fortune 50 company in New York City. A client of ours at the time was number one on Google New York City for personal injury lawyers. It seemed to me at the time a pretty obvious sale, except this was 2007. New York attorneys barely marketed. When they did, it was mainly the Yellow Pages. They were still paying thousands for spots in the Yellow Pages despite most people using the Yellow Pages for booster seats and door stops.

So I started looking at the best salespeople. I realized they were selling with stories. I started to develop a list of stories I could use. I captured three or four Video Case Stories and used these case stories to set appointments. I used Video Case Stories to explain the value of ranking on the first page of Google. I use Video Case Stories to explain the difference between a great website and a bad one. I use Video Case Stories to overcome the skepticism of working with me.

At the same time, YouTube was purchased by Google. They started to rank videos in the Search Engine Result Pages (AKA the SERPS). So, I started to capture my client's stories, rank them, and show the potential of the sales to my clients. Sales skyrocketed.

I used the technique to get in the door. And you know it really hasn't changed. Here is the simple formula.

Do you have X problem, Y problem, or Z problem? Or all of them?

Would you like me to show you how we solve those problems for someone just like you? And now our client has X results and Y transformation. The formula might seem simple.

When you put it all together, it's really hard to say No to these stories, especially when they're on video. New Yorkers are skeptical, to say the least. New Yorkers are hustlers. They assume everyone is stretching the truth. The videos that I created were authentic. The videos helped to overcome many of the objections.

It helped to get me in the door, to get the right presentations in front of them, and to have them believe my prospects and what I said was going to happen. It does work.

This sales structure still works. Mandy Ellefson, whom I work with, coaches Consultants to use this exact process to grow seven-figure consulting businesses. Now she uses LinkedIn and email versus door-to-door sales. I interviewed DOT & Company's founder, Taylor McMaster. DOT & Co is an account management company that does training and fractional account manager placement. Their sales team chooses the appropriate Video Case Story to send their prospects before the sales call. Prospects get on sales calls ready to buy.

Jason Swenk used the Tackle Box Tool we'll introduce and Video Cases Stories to get his salespeople up to speed, making sales within a few days.

Video case stories will improve every step in the sales process. From prospecting to proposals to upsells, PandaDoc is the proposal software company that we use (and they're not sponsoring this at all).

They did a study across all their proposals. They found that videos on proposals close 32% more deals. Look at your proposal right now. Most proposals are not optimized for sales. They are long and boring and often not read. You can simply add the appropriate Video Case Story (or three) and see a 32% increase in sales. That's a nice bump in deals. That should pay for the time you spend on this process.

Having a bunch of testimonials saying "You're great" will never do anything. I kind of get annoyed with them. You need a story. Who is this person? Why should I care? Were their problems really like mine? Was the success what I want? These are the questions you must answer. Video case stories do this. They are the key to a great modern sales process.

Marketing Magic with Video Case Stories

I was talking with one of our clients and another digital agency owner, April Iannazzone. She is a leader in marketing for the Med Spa space. I love working with the best marketers because it allows us to push the limits of this process.

Most of the time, Agencies have to "sell" their services.

April told me that she had a Med Spa owner come and inquire about services. The prospect didn't ask for quotes or comparisons. The prospect said they had watched all her videos on YouTube. They inquired if there was room to work with her. They knew she was the one they wanted to work with. That is the power of video.

I hear this all of the time. A great YouTube strategy really connects you to your ideal customers. Video Case Stories launch the best strategies for this powerful platform.

The #2 Biggest Search Engine Gets You in the #1 Most Used Search Engine. YouTube is the number two search engine. Many people go there for every question. YouTube videos also show up in Google searches, the #1 search engine. This means YouTube yields incredible influence in the decision-making process. I only see that growing as AI-created content drives down trust in the written word.

Here's the scenario. A prospect searches for your service on Google. A video of your client or several clients that tells the story of their transformation, of you helping them overcome their problems, of them getting to where they want pops up. What do you think is going to happen? Prospects are going to click on that video.

YouTube rewards great content by ranking it higher. If the content engages the viewers, Google will display it too. We'll get into the elements of amazing stories that people watch so they rank higher.

Most people trust Google and YouTube more than their families. Few things market more powerfully than someone searching on Google or YouTube for help, and your client is there telling the story of working with you. If it's a great story, viewers will engage, remember it, and most likely, remember you. You are steeped in competition for viewers' attention (and memory). The stories have to stand out and be "sticky" because there's so much out there.

They are doing tons of research. Google recently released a study that said that people encounter a brand 250 to 500 times before deciding on that business. You can look at this as either challenges or opportunities. You can bombard with "brand messages" and be that annoying marketer.

Or you can create great stories in various formats that engage, entertain, and inspire your viewer.

Video Case Stories Rank Higher

Stories rank higher in content because they're more engaging. Engagement means more time on that platform. Video is more engaging than the written word because it engages more senses.

Every platform, from YouTube to Google to LinkedIn, rewards engagement by showing that content more. The better the hooks, attention grabbers, the more people will watch your videos.

The better the story, the more emotion you create, the more people will stay on the video. The more emotionally engaging, the more people will engage the rest of your content and take action.

We'll talk about the science behind this a little later, as well as the method to create the perfect story.

YouTube measures engagement more accurately because they know exactly what the viewer is seeing, when they stop, when they rewatch, and when they drop off, as well as what they do next.

More Leads with the Same Traffic

Traffic is sexy. Ranking is sexy. It's awesome to see those numbers rise. It's also the hardest thing to get right and keep right. Algorithms change, costs rise, and platforms come in and out of fashion.

Your goal is not traffic unless you are an influencer. Your goal is new clients, new customers. You want them to spend more money with you over time. Achieve better results. Your goal is to get visitors to convert faster and convert better.

Video Case Stories will help do this. We already mentioned using them in proposals to increase conversion by 32%.

Customer Stories on home pages increase conversion anywhere from 20-200%.

Your About Us Page is the second most used page on your website. This is where visitors want to hear more from other people talking about you and your business and the stories behind it.

(Conversely, Testimonials pages are very rarely clicked. Further proof, no one wants to see testimonials.)

70% of carts are abandoned. Look at your contact page traffic and compare it to actual contacts.

Your individual blog posts and service pages are great opportunities to say, "This is what you should do, and here's the story of someone we helped doing this."

Your traffic campaigns should go to landing pages. Landing pages with customer story videos convert 30-100% better, depending on the study you read.

Video Case Story Conversion Math's

Option A) The Video Case Story Website Conversion Method

You drive 10,000 visitors to your website a month. That traffic generates 200 leads (2%) conversion rate.

You could have case stories in those five places we discussed above, and each placement increases website conversion by 10% (The low end of the spectrum). That's a 50% increase in conversion. Now you are receiving 300 leads.

Option B) Drive More Traffic

In order to receive 50% more leads on the traffic route, you'll have to generate 50% more traffic. That method is simple.

The CHEAPEST clicks in almost any high value industry are at least $20 and often $100 or more per click.

Let's say you are a paid traffic magician. You have a way to get a $1 click to your website. That means to increase leads and traffic by 50%, you'll have to spend $5000 more per month.

What happens when you stop with paid traffic? Those leads vanish. That's a much less sexy magic trick.

That 50% OR MORE is ONLY if we use Video Case Stories on our website.

Of course, you are going to use them in sales, for increase in organic traffic, and then in the best place...

Marketing follow up.

The Fortune is in The Follow Up

Only 2-4% of your audience is ready to buy right now. That number decreases as the cost and complexity of your services grow.

Video case stories can follow your prospects, telling the stories of your best customers everywhere they go.

I always hear from people that they're afraid to email their list too much. That's because they usually email out promotional content. You need to build an email list and email them regularly. Emailing them testimonials is self-serving. It's boring, and it's bad email. That's the kind of email you don't want to receive.

Emailing compelling, heartwarming stories to inspire your followers. It reminds them of the great work you are doing to help transform lives. Emailing your list does a few very powerful things. Of course, you are following up with them.

1. Emailing your list shows them that you're continuing to do great work.
2. Following up with Video Case Stories reminds those on the fence of what they need to do.
3. Emailing videos inspires and engages your audience, increasing your branding. Stories will also lead to more referrals because your list will see someone as if they are someone they know.
4. The Case stories help your audience to get to know your tribe.

Follow up isn't only for lost leads. I mentioned Dot and Co using Video Case Stories. Video Case Stories transformed sales conversations. You should email relevant stories to all prospects. Every prospect, whether they want to say it or not, wants to hear your clients' stories.

Sending over testimonials impresses no one.

You can email relevant stories after any type of discovery call. You'll know exactly what type of stories because they'll tell you in their call. The Video Case Stories Tackle Box you'll create will make it easy to find these stories in seconds.

Social Media is also a follow up tool. I can't tell you how many prospects have subscribed to our channels, and then recited a recent Video Case Story when they reached out. I almost feel bad for them. They know they should have done these things to get results like that in the Video Case Stories.

Your Best Customer's Telling their Stories EVERYWHERE: Retargeting

Kasim at Solutions 8 is one of the world's best marketers. Solutions8 is ranked one of the Top 1% of Google Ads agencies by Google. We were lucky enough to create their Video Case Stories. Kasim uses them for SEO on YouTube.

"I was surprised by the Organic Lift," said Kasim.

Kasim spent $200,000 **a month** on YouTube ads. The best performing ad? His Video Case Stories.

Kasim's YouTube campaign helped to propel them to the absolute leader in Google Ads.

Retargeting customer stories is the most powerful and underused tool. Retargeting means showing your videos to people who have visited your site, are on your email list, or performed some other action.

They were interested at some level in your service. Now your best customers are telling their stories everywhere on the internet, 24 hours a day, 7 days a week.

In theory, that's powerful. Kasim proved it.

You can't just have testimonials doing that. You need different hooks, angles, and stories.

More "Social" Social Media

Most social media fails because the managers out there forget the social part. They just broadcast. I've always gone by the "What would you do at a party?" route. I don't mean a college craziness drunken pool party. We're talking about a nice dinner party where you are meeting people for the first time.

You wouldn't just broadcast the latest news. You would discuss it. You would ask people about themselves, find something in common, and possibly tell a story.

Great stories make for the best social media. Social media outlets want engagement. Stories provide that. You'll get more engagement. You'll also be remembered.

The benefit of stories is that people will see themselves but be reminded of others. I see Video Case Stories as the most shared content out there.

That is besides puppies, babies, and otters. Those are great for social media but really don't explain your business.

Improve Operations

A woman comes upon three brick layers. The title kind of spoils it. She asks them what they do.

The first one grumbles and says, "I'm laying bricks."

The second one says wholeheartedly, "I'm building a beautiful church."

The third tells her, "I'm playing my part in creating a place that brings together and inspires families and communities."

We all want to feel like the third. We all want to find that type to work with us.

Enter Video Case Stories. You can tell your people that you're doing a great job. You can show them metrics. Your team will still feel disconnected from the results. Seeing the story and feeling the transformation through Video Case Stories inspires people to work at another level. They enjoy their jobs more. They will put out better work.

Video Case Stories help find and retain that top talent. Great people want to be a part of something that makes an impact. You can talk all day to prospective team members about how great your company is, or you can show them the outcome.

You might think, "I don't have those kinds of stories." I guarantee you do. It's all the more reason to go through the process in this book.

Video Case Stories provides a guiding star of what you want your team to accomplish.

Video Case Stories will guide improvements in your operations. You will find out what people REALLY like and don't like. The interview process gets to the heart of their story. You'll identify opportunities to improve your business and create new products and services.

Video Case Stories as a product came from such a story. We were interviewing clients, and time and time again, the Video Case Stories were at the heart of their success. Originally, we were a full-service agency, then a web and video agency. Video Case Stories made the fastest impact, so we focused there. We knew that not from surveys but from listening to our clients.

Almost all of Walt Disney's innovations came from listening to his customers. The Hot Dog wrapper story is a perfect example.

Your customer stories should be at the heart of your operations, your hiring, and your training. To get the latest methods, make sure to click here to subscribe to our YouTube channel. Or go to https://crewstube.com

Scan here for bonus videos on this chapter.

https://linke.to/dSFv0i

4.0 FUNDAMENTALS AND COMMITMENT

Get the fundamentals down, and the level of everything you do will rise.
~ Michael Jordan

You've heard of that Michael Jordan guy, right? In the **Tool Kit,** you'll find a picture of Kobe Bryant, another legend of basketball, and in the picture, he has a broken right hand. He's on the court in pajamas, practicing free throws with his left hand.

Obviously, no one's forcing Kobe at this point to do it, and most would advise him to stay home and rest, but Kobe knows free throws win games. It's not that Kobe was bad at free throws.

Kobe knew he had to practice the fundamentals over and over despite the circumstances. Kobe was not the best player when he started playing basketball. He showed up, worked hard, and developed a consistent, fundamental, committed work ethic like no other.

Most importantly, Kobe did unsexy things when no one was watching. Legend says that after the LA Lakers drafted him, where most players would've celebrated, Kobe hit the court and practiced. He was shooting jump shots and free throws on arguably the biggest night in his life up until then. Kobe committed consistently to the fundamentals. He was an 18-time All Star in the NBA, a level like an elite few. He won five NBA Championships, and it shows you that success is about commitment to the fundamentals, over and over. The fundamentals are not sexy, but they always win.

Practice Tying Your Shoes

Many champions came out of John Wooden's UCLA basketball program. They had ten national titles in eleven years. Wooden started with a below average UCLA team that worked out in horrible, musty, rundown facilities. He turned that around, and Wooden won ten NCAA basketball titles. Every four years, he had all new players. Imagine if your business had to get a completely new team every four years. Every single player started by learning to tie their shoes in John Wooden's UCLA program.

Lew Alcindor, who eventually became Kareem Abdul-Jabar, one of the greatest players of all time, started by learning to tie his shoes correctly during his first days of practice at UCLA. He did it over and over. John Wooden knew that shoes tied properly prevented injuries and blisters and extended their playing time.

Fundamentals, fundamentals, fundamentals. Customer stories are the fundamentals of any business. To do them properly, you need a level of commitment and dedication. There will never be a hair-on-fire moment because case stories are important, not urgent. You might get a big outcome for one of your clients or customers and say, "Hey, let's do a story, but your business will not collapse without them."

Your business will slowly, quietly become average without a commitment to your customer stories, and then eventually, it will become less than average. Of course, there will always be a reason not to do customer stories.

"I'm too busy."

"I'm focused on sales."

"I don't need leads right now."

"I've got a different marketing campaign." *That shiny, bright object out there that can distract you.*

Walt Disney was one of the most famous people in the world the years before his death. He came into everyone's living room once a week through television.

It's hard for me to remember and for some to even imagine, but we all had to sit down and watch the same shows on the same two or three channels at the same time.

Walt came into **everyone's** living room. The opening of Disneyland was the biggest TV event ever at its time. And then, every Sunday, everyone in America — just about every family with a TV — watched.

Walt was one of the biggest stars in the entire world. And it's also hard to understate the expansive impact he had on the world, but that's a completely different book.

The year before his death, Walt was very sick. He eventually died of lung cancer, but he also had kidney issues, and a debilitating polo injury, and had to have his sinuses drained every single week. On top of that, he was a huge star and would often get hounded. He had plenty of reasons to just phone it in the years before his death.

But still, Walt would walk the park despite his illness. And despite all that success, he was still talking to guests, asking questions, and learning their stories. Allegedly, Walt would have people sit and spy on guests to listen to their comments about the park. Walt didn't need to improve anything. Walt knew.

Disney had to continually evolve, though, to be the best. Walt knew the stories of his customers were the key to success, the key to that evolution, the key to his impact. I'm sure listening to all those stories also inspired him in his final days. The habit of collecting, crafting, and delivering stories is what made Walt Disney great.

I can't imagine what Walt would've done with access to the internet. Customer stories, case stories are the most important habit in a business. But to succeed at a unique commitment, you need consistency, and you need to understand the fundamentals. You put all that together, and you've got an unstoppable force in this book. I'm going to give you the fundamentals.

I'm going to give you our exact systems for collecting, crafting, and delivering amazing customer stories on video. I need you to bring the commitment and the consistency. I told these stories because the rest of the book is going to be a textbook. You know, I could write a 300-page treatise on Video Case Stories, and I might someday. But I wanted you to succeed as fast as possible, so I want you to commit and become consistent.

Many won't have read this far, and many won't read past here. But I tell you this—dedicate at least 30 minutes a week to your customer stories. It's not a huge dedication. But we can see how important it is. It is fundamental. Just this practice alone, just taking this time out to dedicate to the stories and using some of the things that I'm going to teach you in this book, will transform your business and your marketing.

You can move faster, you can dedicate more time, and you can get results faster. You can set up a call with a Video Case Story strategist and accelerate the process massively. But even if you hire a Video Case Story strategist and a team, dedicate the time to work with them, dedicate the time to understand how this works, dedicate the time to listening to the stories and using them and reusing them.

Give it a year. Most Won't.

Plan to work on this for a year. Think about Walt; think about Kobe showing up when he's sick, when he's injured, to do the fundamentals. After a year of consistency, you will have the momentum to keep it up as a habit. So right now, go to your calendar and choose a block of time.

I would suggest doing it first thing in the day because we all know it gets easier to put off in the afternoon. So choosing a morning will help to make it a habit and have you clearheaded. It will inspire you if you have to get up an hour early. It's worth it. So put it on your calendar, and then email me your commitment at ian@videocasestory.com.

If you do email me, put in the subject line, "I'm committed." Don't write "Commit me" because I'm just not qualified for that.

Tell me when you are getting started. Tell me the time and date, and I will send you things to inspire you.

I'll send you new techniques, the latest case stories, the latest ways they're working, the latest success stories because inspiration is key. And if you're not looking for ongoing motivation, you should.

Marketing is tough.

Because, like the great Zig Ziglar said (one of my absolute favorite quotes), "People often say that motivation doesn't last. Well, neither does bathing. That's why we recommend it daily."

Before you become a master of YOUR case stories, let's get one thing out of the way once and for all.

Testimonials Stink.

Scan here for bonus videos on this chapter.

https://linke.to/jvPT

5.0 TESTIMONIALS STINK

You keep using that word. I do not think that word means what you think it means.
~ Inigo Montoya, *The Princess Bride*

Words have amazing power. When you ask for testimonials, you think you're asking for customer stories. That's not what you're going to get. Testimonials. Just that word, making them, asking them, producing them, even mentioning them. It's hurting your business. You asked for a testimonial, and what you got — thinking you were going to get a customer story — was something you just really didn't want to use. I've heard that from so many clients. So, let's just go through a few of the problems with testimonials because I know that if we don't get past this, you're going to end up getting the same results you got before.

Reason #1 Testimonials Stink

There are three big reasons that testimonials hurt your business. The number one reason is that when you ask for testimonials, you get someone talking about you. They will talk about you, how great you are. That's not what anyone wants to hear. That's not what anyone wants to remember, and that's not anything that anyone will buy.

You think people buy your why. No one's buying your why. People first buy with their why. Are you going to answer their problems? After they're engaged, they will get into your why, but they still don't buy it. Yes, there's a point where people care about the story of your business. That story still has to be related to them.

We use Video Case Stories to make amazing About Us videos. The "about us" is still "about them." Even then, your audience really just cares about how the story lines up with their story. That's the number one reason testimonials are not powerful — but customer stories are — because testimonials are about you, NOT your prospects and your customers. They want to know stories about someone like them. They want to know the issues that person had and how they overcame them.

Testimonials are about you. Video Case Stories are about them.

Reason #2 Testimonials Stink

Testimonials are not stories. We think in stories. We remember stories. We buy stories. We are transformed by stories. When you ask someone for a testimonial, when you send a videographer out for a testimonial, they might capture a bit of the story. The person that you're interviewing will talk about the outcome. Maybe they'll talk about how happy you made them. Very rarely is there a story. We will be getting into the elements of a powerful story later.

When you don't have a story, you don't have a reason to pay attention. Your prospects don't have a reason to remember that amazing outcome. There are no emotions for someone to be motivated to take the next step. Testimonials rarely give someone a reason to take action.

And that's what we want your customer stories to do — get results. We want them to be remembered. We want them to be engaged. We want people attracted to them and then to take action. Testimonials will never, ever do that because they are not stories.

I was doing a Case Story interview for Build, Grow, Scale, an amazing ecommerce education company. Ane was attending their event and was pulled in for an interview. I could tell she was a little nervous. She did the usual testimonial, "This is great."

Most would have stopped at the testimonial. I knew there was more.

I dug deeper. We started to discuss her background. She had struggled as a graphic designer and entrepreneur before Build Grow Scale.

I asked her what the improvement in her business meant for her. She started to talk about her daughter.

I could see the tears well up in her eyes.

I asked her how her life had changed.

Through tears, she described how she could now provide for her daughter and be an amazing role model.

It's been almost six years.

I'm getting teary eyed right now writing this.

That's a transformation. Simply grabbing a testimonial would have never found that.

Build, Grow, Scale used that story over and over to draw in amazing people and more women into their group.

More than just a big result, more than just a dollar amount, more than just an outcome, your prospects are drawn to transformation.

Here are some transformation examples:

Scared to Courageous

Dying to Healthy

Overwhelmed to In Command

Alone to Connected

Suffering Business to Thriving Enterprise

Testimonials will never have transformations because they are about you. The only way you are going to find the transformations is by digging for the stories.

There is nothing more powerful than the promise of (and delivering of) transformation.

Ask for a testimonial, and you'll never find that amazing story.

Reason #3 Testimonials Stink

Testimonials check the box, and that's it.

So many people, great marketers, come to me and say, "I have customer stories. Can you edit them?" We usually can't. Why? I watch them, and the videos are simply testimonials, someone talking about how great their business is.

These videos use words like "great customer service," "amazing," "relevant results," and "I'd recommend them to anyone." There's no specificity. There's no problem. There's no real emotion. There are no moments. There's no story there, but that business checked the box saying, "We have testimonials."

Walt Disney could have checked the box.

Towards the end of his career, he didn't have to go out and listen to his park-goers' stories.

He didn't have to listen to the stories of the people watching his movies, but he knew how important it was to his business. And he kept doing it. Walt kept using the stories to "Plus" the Disney Empire. The best people listen to the customer stories, collect them, and constantly use them to improve their marketing and improve their business. The best use customer stories to evolve their business.

"Fun" little story: That's why we originally named our business evolveAL-OUD. Worst. Name. Ever. No one can spell it or understand it.

People often ask me:

"Can I just get a list of questions?"

"Can you just send the software?"

"Can't I just, you know, write the testimonials myself?"

No, no, no. When you just collect testimonials, you check the box, and you say, "That's over. I know what people want. I know what they like. I don't need to listen to my customers. I don't need to collect more stories. I don't need to improve my marketing."

You have checked the box and moved on to the next shiny object. You give up your opportunity to connect with your customers. You miss out on finding these amazing Video Case Stories in your business that can transform every part of your business.

Today, I worked with my friend (I won't name him) on his positioning statement. He needed to stand out. He struggled because he did not have customer stories to listen to. Your customers will give you all of the information you need. You just have to listen to their stories. You're giving up on all the amazing opportunities by checking the box.

Testimonials won't help you find new ways to sell new differentiators or improve your positioning. No one's going to watch your testimonials on your YouTube channel, so the testimonials won't get engagement. You won't get the view time. You won't be showing up in different YouTube searches. You definitely won't get into the Google Search results with testimonials.

A testimonial can definitely not be used as cold outreach by your sales team.

"Hey, can I send you a video of someone saying how awesome we are?" No one wants that.

You've also asked your customers to talk about how great you are.

That's just weird. That's really uncomfortable for them, even if they want to say something awesome.

And if you give them a script, man that looks really, really bad.

Trust me.

I see a lot of those commercials here in Orlando, Florida, for personal injury attorneys. These attorneys turn you off. They are the ones making these attorneys look like bad used car salesmen.

These attorneys missed their story. Their stories are the number one tool for marketing your business, sales, and operations.

They checked the box.

You're missing out on those huge opportunities to use those stories to innovate your business. You're missing out on all of this because you checked the testimonial box. You didn't make customer stories a priority.

I don't even like the word because it ends up causing all of these problems. Get focused on Video Case Stories.

Now that you're dedicated, vow you're not going to ask for testimonials. Make a vow. You're not going to use the word testimonials (except to recommend this book).

One thing case stories won't ever do is help you create a Case Story Flywheel, the ultimate tool for scaling a business.

5.1 THE CASE STORY FLYWHEEL: FLYWHEEL FISHING FOR BIGGER FISH, BIGGER PROFITS, EASIER WORK

We've touched on evolving your business with Video Case Stories. Now we delve deeper into the extraordinary potential of the Case Story Flywheel and its ability to revolutionize your business. We'll explore real-world examples of industry leaders who have harnessed the power of the Video Case Story Flywheel to attract bigger clients, achieve remarkable growth, and elevate their services to new heights.

One such success story is Mandi Ellefson, founder of the Hands-Off CEO program. Mandi has successfully guided numerous companies in scaling their businesses and charging premium prices for their services, ranging from $10,000 to over $1 million. By leveraging the Video Case Story Flywheel, Mandi's clients attract better clients through their sales and marketing efforts, create efficient systems around their clients, and continually collect more case stories to market to even bigger and better clients.

Another remarkable example is Jason Swenk, a renowned authority in the agency world. Over a span of seven years, Jason used the Case Story Flywheel to attract bigger agencies as clients. By showcasing the success stories of his agency clients, he was able to demonstrate the value and results they achieved, ultimately attracting larger and more prestigious agencies. Jason charged more, improved his services, and improved his results. The Video Case Story Flywheel played a pivotal role in Jason's journey, propelling him to new heights and positioning him as an influential figure in the industry.

During the editing of this book, we evolved Jason's offer again, releasing his Agency Mastery program. We created a new video series, improved his funnel, the service, and his offer. We were able to 300% increase the number of conversions on his sales calls.

All using Video Case Stories and the Tackle Box as our starting point and guide.

It's not just my clients. The iPhone is the perfect example of the Case Story Flywheel. It all started with the iPod. A great Case Story in just a sentence,

"1000 songs in your pocket." Those stories of the iPod grew their audience. Steve Jobs and the Apple team listened to their audience and evolved into the iPhone. The iPhone has been rocky over and over, but listening to what people really want and iterating grew the Case Story Flywheel. Soon everyone had an iPhone. They also discovered the stories of the App Store and how apps were transforming peoples' lives.

Their commercials were stories of people transforming into health nuts, communications experts, and rockstars using the iPhone. The biggest iPhone transformation for most was from Tech Luddite to Tech Genius.

When we examine the accomplishments of Titans like Jobs and Disney to Mandi Ellefson, Jason Swenk, and countless other service-based businesses, we uncover a common thread—the presence of a Case Story Flywheel.

This powerful mechanism, rooted in storytelling and supported by Video Case Stories, propels businesses toward extraordinary growth and success. It's important to note that the Case Story Flywheel is not limited to video alone; it encompasses any storytelling method that captures and leverages success stories to attract bigger clients, optimize service delivery, and drive positive momentum.

It's a simple but not easy process:

1. Acquire customer
2. Provide amazing service and results
3. Capture that story
4. Identify the parts of the service and the client you like
5. Attract more of those specific people and services
6. Narrow down, improve, and charge more because you're the expert
7. Improve your offering and results
8. Streamline operations for those results
9. Capture bigger stories
10. Use the bigger stories to acquire bigger customers

Over time, you'll find your "hedgehog" move as defined by Jim Collins in the book *Good to Great*

1) What you are deeply passionate about?
2) What you can be the best in the world at.
3) What best drives your economic or resource engine?

You'll have bigger stories and be known for this. Another thing happens: It becomes EASIER to deliver because you are getting more focused.

Revenue rises along with profit margins.

As we embark on this journey of unleashing the power of the Case Story Flywheel, let's acknowledge the transformative impact it can have on our businesses. Whether we adopt Video Case Stories or other storytelling techniques, the fundamental principles remain the same. By harnessing the potential of storytelling, we create a flywheel effect that drives continuous improvement, attracts ideal clients, and fuels the growth of our service-based businesses.

Now, armed with the insights from Mandi Ellefson, Jason Swenk, and countless other success stories, it's time to embrace the Case Story Flywheel and witness its profound impact on our own businesses.

Let us embark on the journey of implementing this powerful mechanism and experience firsthand how it elevates our services, attracts better clients, and propels our businesses toward unprecedented success. The Case Story Flywheel is a natural product of the upcoming Tackle Box process, which we are about to dive into.

Scan here for bonus videos on this chapter.

https://linke.to/CrkR

6.0 THE VIDEO CASE STORY SYSTEM

Each step in the system I'm going to lay out here is critical — important — and it's been set up in a certain way to make sure that you have that success. But you need to be in the right mindset too.

After people ask me how much a video testimonial costs, the next thing they ask is, "What camera should I use?" And then, "Can I get a list of questions?" Then, about a month later, I hear, "Uh, that didn't come out the same."

John Wooden made every player learn to tie their shoes the right way. First, he knew it started with the fundamentals. He knew he had to maintain a system. And just like Wooden did, there's a specific way we found success with case stories.

Shortcuts very often end up in subpar results.

I stress that you cannot simply skip over to the questions and expect the results. I've skipped steps sometimes because I've done this so many times. Every time, I regret it. Each step sets up the next and the ones after. Once you have done it, it's done. Just rinse and repeat. You'll get better and better. Your results will improve. Your business will improve.

Process Overview

Step 1: The GPS: Goals Performance Strategy review. We'll examine your goals. You need to know what results you want. Seems obvious, but most skip this.

Step 2: Review your "Fish in the Barrel." These are the easy places that every business should be using Video Case Stories to close more deals. These are fast opportunities to land those Big Fish that are already swimming around your business.

Step 3: Start The Case Story Tackle Box: We'll make our first pass through the strategy, the Video Case Story tackle box. We'll review the elements of your stories, finding possible keywords, hooks, and angles. We'll create a plan together for asking the right people the right questions. This is the key to collecting amazing Video Case Stories.

Step 4: Design Planning: We'll brainstorm the design of your case stories. Video Case Stories should be more than just interviews to really drive that engagement. We'll discuss graphics, text, b-roll, and versions.

Step 5: We enter the collection phase. In the collection phase, we'll craft the questions, decide what types of interviews to do, go through interviewing techniques, and properly set up interviews.

Step 6: The CSI process: After collecting the interviews, we'll do a deep dive into each interview — what we call a CSI or a case story investigation — to find all the ways that you can use the videos, all the ways you can use the information we found there.

We'll discuss the length of the videos, different formats, structure of the videos, and elements that you should include. We'll decide where they should be distributed once we get the videos completed. The distribution strategy informs the production process.

Step 7: Post-production: This is how we edit and create all the different types. It's a process that's streamlined to create the perfect content.

Step 8: Distribution Time! We'll review the essential platforms and places, including your "Fish in The Barrel" checklist. This will be an "evergreen" overview, focusing on high level strategy. Except for YouTube, we'll dive deeper into that because It's going to be here for a while.

Step 9: Becoming the Best Storyteller: The Best Storyteller Wins: We'll discuss actually using Video Case Stories to create other videos, improve your current content, your website content, and all of your other marketing operations.

I know at this point, it's going to be really, really tempting to jump to the part that you feel like you need the most help with. Make sure to tie your shoes first. Make sure to go through this entire system. I want you to have as much success with Video Case Stories as quickly as possible.

Scan here for bonus videos on this chapter.

https://linke.to/WH9zBE

7.0 THE CASE STORY TACKLE BOX

In the quest to capture the proverbial "Big Fish," it is essential to approach the task strategically, much like you would if you were embarking on an actual fishing expedition.

Consider this scenario: If you're going fishing, you wouldn't just haphazardly hop onto a boat. Instead, you would formulate a plan. You'd need to identify the types of fish you're after because this would dictate where you should cast your line. You'd need to know the optimal time for fishing, the frequency of your trips, the kind of boat required, and, of course, the equipment to pack. In fishing terms, you'd fill up a tackle box — for non-anglers, that's a container where you store your hooks, lures, and lines.

The same logic applies when you're trying to reel in Big Fish through video marketing. You shouldn't just randomly venture onto a platform without a plan devoid of compelling content or compelling stories. Rather, you need to devise your narrative in advance, store it in a dedicated location, and ensure it's ready for deployment when you embark on another quest for a big catch. You need to be acquainted with your arsenal — your hooks (the catch points in your story), angles, keywords, and the various narratives at your disposal. That's where the Video Case Story Tackle Box comes into play.

The Video Case Story Tackle Box is a tool designed to facilitate planning. It allows you to gather your stories, set objectives, identify your "fish in the barrel" strategy for immediate results, and organize all your narratives. It helps you recognize hooks, angles, keywords, and patterns in positioning. Moreover, it enables you to discern the platforms most beneficial for your campaign and create a structured list of where your stories are being utilized.

You can get access to the Video Case Story Tackle Box via the toolkit found at www.Testimonialbook.com/toolkit.com.

Here, you can download the most recent version. We will guide you through all the steps necessary to populate this toolkit. I also recommend conducting regular reviews of your Video Case Story Tackle Box, perhaps monthly or, at the longest interval, quarterly. This practice will keep you on track, improving your marketing, sales, and operations, as well as helping you assess which stories you've collected, which ones you need to accumulate, and where they're being utilized.

Now, let's dive in and start filling out your Video Case Story Tackle Box!

Scan here for bonus videos on this chapter.

https://linke.to/ligq

8.0 GOOOOALS

You know, you've gotta be very careful if you
don't know where you are going,
because you might not get there.

~ Yogi Berra

I have a friend; let's call him Mit. He tells stories. The stories start out great, but then he kind of piles another story on and then another. The stories become long and tough to follow. We'll be ten minutes in and forget the original story. Why does Mit go into the story without a real point to it or an outcome he wants to achieve? I can't just click away from my friend when I'm sitting there. People can easily click away from your videos. And in fact, even if the story's okay, they're going to click away from the videos. Video case stories can help every part of your business, but trying to get them to help every part of your business at once will lead to failure.

Marketing is a tough game when you know EXACTLY what you want people to do, and they WANT to do it. For example, how many people have you seen push a door that says "Pull" on it? They want to go inside. The marketing of "Pull" is super simple and obvious, and everyone wants the same thing. People push when they should pull because of distraction. That's why your marketing needs to be SUPER goal oriented.

We live in a very distracted era, where people are not sure of what they want, but they want it easy, and they want it now. People want to be entertained. It's a huge task to get any type of marketing to do anything if you don't know exactly what you want it to do. I know that seems obvious, but the keyword is "exactly."

Over my 17 years of marketing experience, I've talked to so many people about their goals. They say, "Oh, I just want more leads," or "I want more business." They are not sure of the exact service they want to provide. Most are not sure of exactly who they want to serve and their problems.

You need to know specifically who you want, what you want to do for your business, and how you want to transform your business. You also need to know who you want to serve to do this. We all like different people.

It's okay to start with one type of Video Case Story. That will make it much easier to have success with them. Then you can move from one goal to the next, to the next, shaping the right stories, and then, where you want to distribute them depends on those goals. You need to sit down and figure out your goals. There are a lot of great books on setting goals. I'm going to give you a crash course into some of my favorite ways.

10-year goals

One of my favorite pieces of advice is from my client and mentor, Gino Wickman, the creator of the Entrepreneurial Operating System.

Gino says, "We greatly underestimate what we can do in ten years and overestimate what we can do in a year." You want to make sure that everything you do from here on out is serving those goals. Otherwise, it's easy for the stories to go in this direction and that.

And like my friend Mit, you'll end up being a bad storyteller. Now your ten-year goal, even your two-year goal, even your one-year goal, can morph over time and change, but you need a guiding light. And then, once you get that, we'll bring it back down to all the things we need to do in the next 90 days. Part of it should be installing a Video Case Story plan.

Goals for the Next 90 Days

The next 90 days are about getting into a rhythm of collecting, crafting, and delivering customer stories throughout your business and your marketing. You don't need to get it all done. You just need to create a rhythm. And then we will talk later on about creating a flywheel where it becomes easier and your business improves rapidly, moving towards those goals.

Campaign Performance and Strategy Goals

Now, once we get specific with the goals and the specific outcomes we want, then we'll look at the various elements of your marketing: the different platforms, where your ideal clients are, the different marketing campaigns you're already running, the marketing campaigns that you want to run. Each part of the marketing campaign has a place where Video Case Stories will fit in.

If you're currently running, say, a pay-per-click campaign, Google Ads, there are various elements, from the ad itself to the landing page, to the checkout page, to the follow-up funnels. All these are places that we can improve with Video Case Stories, but we want to try one at a time. So, on top of that, we also want to look at your other goals.

Service, Pricing, and Profit Goals

Your goals could be raising your pricing to increase profits. Maybe there's a specific type of client or a specific market that you want to move into. Your other goals could include hiring a better team. Whatever those goals are, we need to choose two to three of them immediately that are serving those ten-year goals.

It could be bigger clients. It could be better clients. It could be charging more. It could be higher profits. It could be a lot more clients. Whatever it is, it'll be much easier to decide that if you have those ten-year goals.

I know the ten-year goal can seem daunting, but as I said, it can change. But if you don't get started today with that vision, you're not going to have the outcome you want with the Video Case Stories. I'm not asking you to be completely clear on that ten-year goal, but you can start right now and choose those two to three goals that are going to serve it this year.

I know you want to wing it. I know you want to move forward. I know you came to this book looking for the Big Fish. At this point, you want your marketing, sales, website, thought leadership, and your market share to grow all at once.

You want a high performing sales funnel, but looking at your ten-year goals, you'll be able to say which of these you need to get there the fastest, which is going to have the biggest impact right now and moving forward.

Luckily for you, though, I have the place where every business should start, and you can start before you COMPLETELY have your goals in line.

I've created a strategy to close more referrals, close more leads from your current campaigns, and capture lost deals. The strategy lands more of those fish, those Big Fish that are already swimming around your business. For that reason, it's called the Fish in the Barrel Strategy.

Scan here for bonus videos on this chapter.

https://linke.to/fm0LRG

9.0 FISH IN THE BARREL

I live on a lake, and I really like to fish (in case you haven't noticed by all the metaphors) and cruise around on my pontoon boat. If you want to see some awesome sunset pics, you can check out I Love Lake Life (i_love_lakelife) on Instagram . My son Max has grown to really like fishing as well.

He's just not a fan of cruising around on the pontoon boat. When friends come over, they do want to go out. They want to go out on the lake and try and catch the big bass. Bass fishing is tough. It's especially tough to land the Big Fish.

You need the right time of day. You need to find the right spot and the right depth. You have to find the right lure and know how to present it. You have to have the right place and the right gear. A lot of catching the Big Fish is luck. There's a lot of skill to it too. As any great angler will tell you, it's a combination of all those factors. Then you need to get right in front of the right bass. When the bass tastes it, you've got to set the hook.

It's kind of like going out fishing for clients. Statistics say only 2-4% of prospects are ready to buy right now. You have to make sure you are in front of them with the perfect hook when they're ready. And I do literally mean hook, which we'll talk about more soon. *Just not the same type of hook we're using to catch the bass. That would be weird.*

Max quickly learned that we had all sorts of fish around our dock. We started to feed them. They became hungry around the dock and were easily caught. These weren't all bass. He would catch up to 20 of these small fish in an hour. These fish started to actually attract the big bass.

Those bass became excited. Catching them became easier. All of a sudden, we weren't spending so much time casting. While not catching fish all over the lake, Max, the not so expert fisherman, was landing fish right off our dock.

This is what's happening in your business right now. You have referrals that might not be calling you, or if they do call you, they're not convinced because your online presence doesn't speak to them.

You're not spending enough time tending to the opportunities right in front of you. Maybe they contacted you and ghosted you. You have leads that you're not following up with as well as you could. For many of you, I know your social media presence isn't very social. Look at your website traffic. A good conversion rate is 4% of visitors. I'm guessing you are around 2%. There are Big Fish swimming around your business. You are not landing them because you want the fanciest new lure. You're not focusing on The Fish in The Barrel.

You want to go out through the internet and test out those new platforms, thinking that that's what's going to land the Big Fish. Meanwhile, you're neglecting those fish all around your dock, what we call the Fish in the Barrel. ("Fish near the dock" just didn't have the same ring to it.)

You want them to remember you. You most likely don't have stories that stick out and are memorable, those 96% of people who are going by your website, going by your web presence. Big Fish are going by not ready to buy right now. They just swim away, forgetting all about you.

How many websites do you leave that you want to remember but can't? The websites that I forget about: Enough questioning if I had too much fun in college . . . or maybe I'm just getting a little too old. There are about a dozen points that every business should be concentrating on to land those Big Fish swimming right around them. Video case stories are the perfect way to land the fish in your barrel.

Overcoming the Google Effect

There's a host of cognitive biases that we'll explore in-depth over time - you can subscribe to my YouTube channel for regular updates. One of the most recent discoveries we'll be discussing is called the Google effect, a testament to the brain's inherent laziness.

In essence, the brain is an energy-conserving organ that doesn't want to expend more effort or resources than necessary. It's also a rapid adapter, as evidenced by our emerging understanding of the Google effect.

Nowadays, it seems like I'm forgetting more and more. Whether it's due to aging, losing brain cells, or inadequate nutrition, the phenomenon is widespread. However, many researchers attribute it to the Google effect. Our brains, they argue, are not retaining information, especially from the internet, because they don't have to - Google is always at our fingertips. How often do you find yourself unable to recall a word, a sentence, or the meaning of something? This is a common occurrence for many, including myself.

For you, the implications of this trend are significant, particularly if you've invested heavily in SEO and PPC to boost rankings and traffic. To maximize the return on that investment, you must ensure your traffic is "sticky." Given that conversion rates hover between 2% and 4%, the chances of a visitor remembering your brand are diminishing. This is especially true if your company name is long and complicated, like many law firms, unconventional, or exceedingly common.

The importance of captivating stories becomes glaringly obvious in this context. Without them, even if you rank number one, there's little chance of a visitor remembering your brand unless they need your services immediately and you manage to convert them. Therefore, this "fish in the barrel" strategy is critical as the Google effect intensifies, causing people to remember less and less about our internet marketing.

A Few of the Fish in the Barrel Uses

The Fish in the Barrel Strategy will improve every business website.

Reminder: You can get the Fish in The Barrel Checklist and Calculator in the tool kit at www.Testimonialbook.com/toolkit.com.

Your homepage is a great place for Video Case Stories. This is where it's key to call out the problem and the solution. You can't just have "Jill loves my company." Who is Jill? Why does she love your company? What was her problem? Testimonials don't solve this. Video Case Stories will.

I see so many people put testimonials on there. Testimonials won't get the clicks. When you go to a homepage, you want to know if the services are right for you. You're not really worried about what someone says about how great a person is. That's the opportunity to have case stories on your homepage, featuring the problems and the transformation, using the hooks that we're going to talk about to draw them in to view the videos.

A big, missed opportunity on websites is creating an incredible and *converting* About Us page. This page is generally the second most used page on most websites. Prospects, at this point in the journey, want to like and trust you. There's no better way for prospects to like and trust you faster than other people talking about their experiences of working with you. Place your Video Case Stories on your Services page on your website. It should have Video Case Stories specific to that service.

Did you know that 70% of online shopping carts are abandoned? That is just a form. I bet if you look at the traffic for your Contact Us page, you're probably getting three or four contacts per 200 visits. Video Case Stories will help to convert those Contact Us visitors and remind them why you are awesome. This is the point that people are ready to work with you.

We'll discuss other videos created using the Video Case Story footage, like the About Us, the Process Video, and Brand Overviews.

Email Out Your Video Case Stories Often

Email engagement series should be sent with every opt-in and every sales opportunity. Opt-in for the Tool Kit at www.Testimonialbook.com/toolkit.com and you'll see our series. *Make sure to reply to the first email so you don't miss it!*

DOT & Co, the account management service we discussed earlier, uses their Video case stories in email engagement with new prospects. This is exactly how they increased the effectiveness of their sales calls. You should follow up with multiple stories, emails, long-term nurturing for those prospects you either missed or who were just not ready.

Emailing nurture campaigns with Video Case Stories reminds your current clients of the success that you're having. This will frame their current situation in a better light. You will also increase the number of referrals, increase more spending with them, and increase the trust in their current services. Your online reputation is a critical place for Video Case Stories. You need to be ranking case stories for your name. When someone Googles your name, it's an easy way for them to find customers talking about how great their experience was with you.

Optimize for your Name in the #2 Most Used Search Engine

I don't like to be platform specific in this book because I want it to be evergreen. I want it to be something that you can come back to. I don't see YouTube and Google going anywhere soon. So we'll talk a little bit about them as part of your Fish in the Barrel Strategy. YouTube is the number two most used search engine.

It's also the place where people spend more time than Netflix. My son watches YouTube on our home TV. His generation will watch it more and more. The generations before us are watching it. Everyone is watching YouTube. People are more likely to consume the rest of your content on YouTube, especially once they visit your profile and see your stories. We'll talk a little bit later about how to get better ranking YouTube videos, but your case stories should be on your YouTube page, like a homepage.

People are going to go there to find out more about you. YouTube is also one of the most discoverable platforms. You get both intention, a search for knowledge, and answers. You also can draw attention because people are there, and you can grab their eye.

Unsexy Wins: Tie Your Shoes, Shoot the Free Throws, Catch the Fish in The Barrel

Now, catching the fish in the barrel isn't sexy. People like to go out and do the hard thing, right? I'm guilty of that as well. We want to go out, scout the open waters, and land that Big Fish.

It's a rush. You won't necessarily get that rush with the Fish in the Barrel Strategy. Just like you won't get that rush by tying your shoes properly before the basketball game, you won't get that rush practicing free throws, but you will achieve success. The Fish in the Barrel Strategy can easily 10X increase your initial investment in Video Case Stories.

Whether you work with one of our specialists or you do it yourself, whether it's a time investment or you pay someone, The Fish in The Barrel strategy will 10X your investment in Video Case Stories. After that, everything else you do is icing on the cake. But don't take my word for it. I created a calculator.

You can get the calculator at www.Testimonialbook.com/toolkit.com

I also created a mini course you'll be able to access that explains the Fish in The Barrel Strategy.

The Undeniable Math of The Fish in the Barrel Strategy

So let's do a quick calculation. Video Case Stories can last for a long time. On average, the Video Case Stories we create — when they're done using this process — last at least four years. One of our dental clients has been using the same Video Case Stories for over 12 years. Let's assume four years on the low end. If you want to skip over this, you can, but this is pretty easy math. Also assume you have a lifetime client value (LCV) of $10,000.

Use the Video Case Stories in 10 of the 12 places that we have right now. Once a year, you convert one more client from each placement.

That equals ten more clients a year because of Video Case Stories. The Video Case Stories are there for four years.

That's 40 more clients. At $10,000 per client, that's a $400,000 return on investment, and that's not including landing the bigger fish because you have a stronger online presence. That's not including the increase in traffic that you're going to get to your website. That's not including using this in outbound sales or using this in your contracts and in your proposals.

Here's the Math

10 Placements x 1 Client Per Year x $10,000 LCV x 4 Years = $400,000 ROI from the Fish in the Barrel Strategy.

That's just from your current marketing efforts and improving them using the Fish in the Barrel Strategy. That return on investment *does not include* having more authority, being able to make clients close easier, or being able to charge more because of your Video Case Stories.

That's a very conservative lifetime value for most service-based businesses or software as a service, SaaS.

$400k ROI is a sexy number.

It's just not a sexy tactic.

You are missing out on opportunities every day by not having Video Case Stories in these places.

Scan here for bonus videos on this chapter.

https://linke.to/vz1r4

10.0 LET YOUR BIG FISH LEAD YOU TO MORE

If you ever hired a fishing guide, you know that they have secret spots where the fish are biting. These spots are so valuable that most guides will go to great lengths to protect them. To prevent you from sharing or returning, they won't even let you have a GPS or your phone out while you're traveling there.

Fish tend to hang out in the same spots. Just like at my dock, the average fish often attracts bigger fish. It's the same with humans. We are attracted to people who are similar to us and have similar interests or to people that we look up to.

This is memetic desire, one of the most powerful forces of motivation in humans. It can fall under a cognitive bias, like the Google Effect. Memetic desire, by definition, is desire according to a model or according to another person. It is a form of imitation, and those models are people like us in our social circles. They are people we want to be like. And it is absolutely one of the biggest driving factors in human decisions.

We see it everywhere. It's most prevalent in teenagers, but you see it in any social circle. People dress alike, talk alike, do the same things, and make the same decisions. **You can control memetic desire.** The way you control it is by modeling or showing. We do that through Video Case Stories. When you identify your ideal clients, you are harnessing this power of attraction. Your Big Fish will attract other Big Fish.

I know this seems controlling. I assume you are doing something that is changing the world for the better. If you help someone grow their business and feed their family. If you help people lose weight and be healthier. If you create software that makes businesses and lives better. You should be doing what you can to get people to take actions that improve themselves.

The flip side is there are people doing bad things using these same techniques. If you want to make the world a better place, you have to admit the real state of the world. Okay, off my soap box.

To mimic your perfect clients, you have to decide why they are your favorites. Decide which clients are your best. Everyone talks about ideal clients, but really, who are your perfect customers? When I go through a Case Story Tackle Box with people, many times, they come into it with either a demographic or possibly an avatar. Most businesses haven't clearly talked through their actual customers and what is powerful about them. So the first step is to identify the clients you enjoy working with the most.

When we do that in our Case Story Tackle Box sessions, we talk about which clients you look forward to having meetings with and which clients your team's excited to interact with. You want to think about which clients are the most profitable. You have to think about those clients that bring in revenue. You also have to review the profits from the project.

Instead of just focusing on getting bigger, better clients and duplicating their characteristics, let's talk about who your actual best clients are. So to get started, we'd list 10 to 15 of your best clients and rate them on factors, including ease of working with them, profitability, referral, and potential enjoyment of the project itself.

Once we do that, we look at those factors and rank them. Now at this point, we want to have as many people in our Case Story Tackle Box as possible. We do want to rank our best clients. This is because we want to know who they are and be able to spend a little more time and effort on collecting the case stories. After we've done this identification process, we'll then dive into their stories and learn about them, what motivates them, and the elements of their story. This exercise will help you further refine your ideal client avatar and attract more of those Big Fish for your business.

Scan here for bonus videos on this chapter.

https://linke.to/CgawS

11.0 THE STORY PREVIEW

In the end, we'll all become stories.
~ Margaret Atwood

It's your big day in court. You're sitting there. Your business supplies sales and marketing to other businesses. One of your vendors tried to buy you out in the middle of the night after you said, "No." They stole all your salespeople.

And now that vendor and their people are on the witness stand. Your lawyer is about to get up and question them.

This is one of the biggest moments in your business, and it can mean life or death to your business.

How would you feel if your lawyer wasn't even there?

How would you feel if that paralegal just printed out some questions from the internet?

You'd be pretty upset because you know that the result will be nowhere as good as if they had spent time knowing who they were going to question, knowing the questions that they wanted to ask, and knowing where they wanted the conversation to go.

Yet when you just print questions from the internet for your case stories, which are crucial to your business, and ask some random person or videographer to go interview your clients, that is exactly what you are doing. Now that we've identified our ideal clients, we want to break down their stories.

We want to know each part of the story that we want to go after, that we want to ask questions about, where we want to dig deeper. I can't tell you how many times I've conducted case story interviews in the past — before this strategy — only to finish and have the client ask, "How was it? Did they talk about X?"

"Uh, no, they didn't. You never mentioned that."

It's tough to ask the person to sit back down at that point and ask that question again without losing the thread of the conversation, and that's the primary reason why we do this exercise. The second reason that we do the connection, conflict, and conclusion exercise is to identify positioning patterns, which we will discuss later.

Each story contains three essential parts. Connection, conflict, and conclusion. There are bigger story equations out there, but you can have a real story with only these three parts. Each story has almost infinite answers for each of these, and we want to identify the ones that we are looking for before the interview. We want to know as much about the story before we ask about the story.

Connection

We need viewers to connect with the subject of the story. There are two goals with connection. First, we want the person to say, "Oh, this person is a lot like me. I get them. I like them." This is why we want to set goals ahead of time and think about our ideal clients. Will this connection point matter to them? It is crucial because no matter what business you're in, it's going to vary.

For digital agencies, it might be the type of business that they're serving. It also might be the type of person that they're serving. People want to know how long that person has been in business, what type of business they have, what's unique about their business, and why <u>this</u> specific piece of software.

Personality types matter to life coach clients.

Health history matters to healthcare clients. (Of course, you must always be HIPPA compliant.)

Never underestimate the importance of small details and connection.

One of my favorite clients was Wayne O'Bryan. He was a personal injury attorney in Richmond, Virginia. He was a brilliant, brilliant marketer, and before being a personal injury attorney, he actually was in the Virginia State Legislature. He ran and won, never having held an office before. And how did he do it?

Wayne went door to door and talked to the people.

He didn't say, "Hey, I'm Wayne O'Bryan, please vote for me." He asked the person about themselves. When Wayne found something in common, he would say, "Oh, I do that too. I'm just like you." Then he would reiterate his name, Wayne O'Bryan, and remind them that he was running for office. Wayne ended up winning.

People will connect with your subject sometimes because of geography or sometimes because of school. One person hired my client because an aunt had the same name as the Video Case Story Subject. Don't underestimate the small details because the small details build up to a bigger picture.

Next, when painting a picture of a person's life in your story, it's important to tap into their emotions to create a connection. For example, you could mention how much they love spending time with their family, how much they love making memories on lake trips, how much they relax playing golf, and all they want to do is play golf. These are all incredibly important aspects of building a complete person's story that we want them to tell.

You won't have time to use a big connection scene in short versions. In longer versions, you'll help people connect with your case stories on a much deeper level. You want them to know, like, and trust the subjects of your stories, and that's where connection comes in because when you have a great connection, they will pay much, much more attention.

Conflict

Humans are naturally drawn to conflict. We can't resist looking at whatever causes a traffic jam, even if it's just a small flat tire on the road. Conflict grabs and holds attention. Attention is the most valuable commodity in marketing.

The stickiest television shows use conflict like a musical instrument, grabbing our attention and keeping us hooked until the next episode. The more problems you call out, the more tension and action you will create. This is why before and after pictures are so effective. Showing someone looking great may not be enough to engage you. You want to see how fat and unhappy they were.

When you see the picture of the person before and how much pain they were in, how unhappy they were, you feel their pain and empathize with them. You are driven to take action. It is those problems that people will pay attention to and relate to. We want to talk even deeper about those problems because it might just be that they're heavy or overweight, but what is that causing? The problem causes them to not have great relationships. It could cause them to hate their clothes. It's causing health problems and more. What are those problems causing?

You want to identify this conflict ahead of time so we can dive deeper into it. You need to ask questions of the subjects. You cause them to travel back and think about those problems. You'll pull out more emotions. Emotions create amazing stories. You need to drive them with pain as long as you provide a true service that's life-transforming. It's our job to be the best marketers possible, and the best way to do that is to remind them of the pain. Pain makes viewers take action. When identifying conflicts in your story, it's also crucial to get as specific as possible.

Paint as much detail into the picture of the problem. Describe the scene, the issues, and the subsequent issues in detail. Specificity creates the picture in the viewer's brain and draws the viewer further into the story. Afterward, you will also want to get as many visuals as possible, taking advantage of the video format.

Every problem has layers. Find and pull out the details of each one. For example, a business problem could include issues with lead generation, which leads to website issues, email issues, messaging issues, follow-up issues, profitability issues, fear of losing the business, fear of not being able to pay your team.

You need to understand that a legal problem or a car accident is not just a single problem; it includes a range of health problems such as various injuries, medical bills, issues with work, childcare, and providing for their family. When talking to clients, it's important to ask about the problems that they've tried to solve and the over-the-counter solutions they've tried.

You want to identify the problems of working with your industry. Marketing with them brings better clients who have tried other solutions and appreciate the value of someone who provides a high level of service, expertise, and authenticity.

Specificity is crucial in identifying conflicts in your story, and once you've identified these conflicts, it's important to draw out the stories and the pain and layer them on to create a satisfying conclusion and transformation that resonates with your audience.

Conclusion

In the conclusion of their story, you'll discuss how things ultimately played out. Did you achieve the results you were after, and if so, what were the metrics that you used to measure their success?

If you're a law firm, for example, we want to know the state of the settlement and how long it took to reach a resolution.

You'll also dive into and discuss the transformations.

For example, in a divorce, yes, they got the divorce. No one's happy after a divorce, but what does it look like three months down the road, six months down the road, nine months down the road? What is the business like now that you turned it around?

This is why we want to also ask for case stories often. And in the long term, we want to know how you helped clients and what metrics you used to measure their success and their progress. Before getting to the conclusion, however, it's important to outline the steps you took to get there.

This process is the key to the story and should be detailed. We want to detail it in the eyes of the client so that they can show what it looks like to work with you. Towards the end of this book, I will briefly touch on process videos. Video Case Stories will help you to make better videos. Process videos are one of the most important videos for converting prospects. Process videos inherently improve traffic conversion, increase your authority, and get better results for your clients.

Finally, transformation is what we're all looking for in a great story. As I mentioned, we want to know how the person's life or the person's business transformed as a result of your work. This is the moment when the story really shines, and we want to know all the details. Did the person achieve redemption or undergo a cathartic event? Pay attention to your favorite movies. You'll notice in the best movies, almost all the characters have some point of redemption. Dig deep here because we want to ask the right questions to uncover the full extent of the transformation.

The connection, the conflict, the process, the conclusion, and the transformation will make for a compelling story that truly engages your audience. And we want to be prepared to do this because this will also help us define better positioning, find hooks, find angles, and obviously collect the best story possible.

Scan here for bonus videos on this chapter.

linke.to/3cdUE5

12.0 POSITIONING PATTERNS, HOOKS, AND ANGLES

The best fishermen know what fish they are looking for, which we decided in the previous chapter. Now that we know the Big Fish, we need to plan to get the hooks and angles that will attract them and land them. Put all your angles together, and you have your positioning statement.

Hooks are the "Attention Grabbers" that make someone pay attention to your positioning statement.

What makes your business different? Is it great customer service? Better product experience? Your team? Just some widget? I've walked into so many businesses that ARE different, and they start to describe what makes them different. It's plain, and it's boring, and it doesn't stand out.

I've looked at thousands of lawyers' websites, and almost all of them say, "Experienced results, relationships. We're there when it matters." Then the law firm is three last names (or more). No one is going to pay attention to that. They are definitely not going to remember you.

Five hundred times and above are the number of exposures to a brand before a decision is made.

Ninety-eight out of 100 website visitors leave without contacting you.

The Google Effect erodes our memories daily.

Positioning makes you stand out and be remembered. Positioning must transcend words. Positioning must be backed by stories.

Think about a time when you just knew something was right for you. A car. A house. A weight loss strategy. That's positioning. It makes a solution the perfect solution for one person. Positioning is a promise made by stories.

Enter the Video Case Story Process.

"Customer Service" is an angle. You can live or die by it. That statement means nothing without a story behind it.

We find great positioning through the planning. Great positioning comes in through the collection of stories, reviewing and massaging them. Video Case Stories come in throughout the entire process. They create positioning with different angles and different hooks of why you are so much better for that person than your competition.

Video Case Stories will position you to eliminate competition and land the Big Fish. Competition anglers (fishermen) come ready for the situation with the best hooks. They don't wait until they are on the water. Your positioning will grab people's attention when we find great hooks to accompany the angles.

Planning for these comes before the stories. We must know the angles we seek. That comes in the Case Story Tackle Box Process.

Let's begin to plan that out ahead of time so that we can find the right angles and great hooks. Great stories make you stand out in this highly crowded, highly competitive marketplace. So that's why we've developed this entire tackle box strategy. Most people go into marketing to develop their positioning. I've seen these marketing meetings. Tables full of executives, stakeholders, and "marketing geniuses" meeting hours upon hours. They have circular talks. They stand there and decide what makes them different, what makes them stand out. And every round, that positioning statement becomes more and more bland.

You know who really needs to be in these marketing meetings and almost never is? Who is the most important person to give insight into your positioning? Of course, you know who that is by now, Your customer. Your clients will give you the best positioning statements. You just have to listen.

It's amazing to me that people don't start with their customer stories in every piece of marketing, but especially in these giant positioning statements. You should be listening to your customers, really interviewing them. You think you might know what they're thinking, but you might be missing positioning patterns before you even get started. That's why we start with planning and talking out our stories.

Every time I start to go through the tackle box, before even interviewing customers, we find new positioning patterns there. There are themes you are overlooking because you are too close to your service. What are positioning patterns? Positioning patterns are concepts and angles that line up.

When you have multiple client stories in front of you, patterns emerge. That's why we start with between five and ten stories in our first tackle box session. You might think that it's customer service that your customers love. The positioning pattern might reveal the insights you provide during that customer service to help you stand out.

You might also find that you have a completely new and different angle that you are missing out on. So many opportunities come out of just talking through the stories and finding patterns. One client realizes that they have a niche in a specific type of nonprofit. Another client starts to develop a niche within a very specific financial sector. I've found so many hooks and angles.

You will find things that help you stand out just by talking about your customers. You help develop new products, services, and new lines of business. Having a third party review your customer stories with you, especially a marketing trained one, helps identify new and deeper positioning patterns before you even go to collect them. And why is this important?

Because we want to know where to dig deep. We can ask about specific angles. A client of ours has such a high level of customer service that they text their clients directly. We found that out in the tackle box. We could have missed that. The interviewee might not think anything of that. We know to ask about that and what that means to them. Now you're on the lookout for hooks. Marketing is about grabbing and holding attention. Hooks grab attention, and then a great story holds attention by building value.

You can build value in your stories in various ways. You can get people to take action. You can build your authority. You can accomplish all those goals that we've talked about. But if you are not grabbing attention and holding it, that means nothing. Hooks are the key to that. They are the key to grabbing and holding attention.

One of my favorite hooks we found for the customer service angle was when we asked for an example of that customer service. During an interview for a case story, the interviewee said, "Watch this." He called the business, and the owner picked up on two rings.

"Hey, how are you?" cam over the speakerphone, demonstrating amazing customer service from the owner. We captured that on video.

"Watch this," is an amazing hook. That grabs any viewer's attention. especially when a customer says that. The hook supports the "fast, personalized customer" service. You'll have a tough time beating that hook with even the best copywriting. We never would have found that hook without the Case Story Tackle Box planning.

Hooks make the best marketing. They make the best subject lines. Hooks make the best intros to any video, including your case stories. Hooks make people pay attention to About Us videos, Brand videos, video blog posts, and your YouTube videos. Ask any creator. They'll tell you how much they work and test hooks.

One of the most prolific labels ever in music is Motown Records.

The backup band of Motown, the Funk Brothers, played on more #1 songs then the Beatles, Beach Boys and Elvis COMBINED.

What was the secret? Hooks.

There's a great documentary on it called "Hitsville,".Barry Gordy and Smokey Robinson, the founders of the , describe how much they invested in the songs' hooks. The entire team at Motown spent days on the first five to ten seconds of those songs. The results speak for themselves. You have one of the greatest song catalogs of all time, from "I Heard It Through the Grapevine" to "Mercy Mercy Me." I bet you immediately get those hooks popping into your head.

That's how important hooks are.

The more great hooks you can find, the better your marketing will be.

Every aspect of your marketing will improve with more hooks. And now, not only have we planned out the hooks that we look for, but you'll have a place to put them. We'll show you exactly how we identify the hooks, how we categorize them, and how we place them in a tackle box so that you have them at a moment's notice.

Positioning is everything. Positioning makes you stand out.

Start planning your positioning before you go into your customer stories. You'll then find patterns. You will find positioning patterns that will identify the angles, those concepts that'll help you to stand out. Then when you have great hooks to reinforce those concepts, you become unstoppable, especially because these are videos of your customer stories and not just writing. So there's no way anyone can steal that from you. No way anyone is going to take your positioning and make it theirs. And this is all before we even get started with the first interview.

Scan here for bonus videos on this chapter.

https://linke.to/JD3Gb

13.0 HOW TO SET UP THE CASE STORY INTERVIEW

Making a film is like putting out a fire with sieve.
There are so many elements, and it gets so complicated.
~ George Lucas

All of this lead up is critical because actual production is so variable. Most films start preproduction years before filming starts.

Hopefully, you agree by now, Customer Stories are the lifeblood of your business. They deserve this level of planning and commitment.

The collection phase is a process that seems straightforward. It's actually filled with nuance that we've discovered over the years.

The systems of knowing

- How to set it up
- Where to set it up
- How to ask the interviewee
- Scheduling and expectations
- Creating great questions
- Great interviewing skills

The "ask" process frames the conversation properly to capture their story, setting it up, and then interviewing to find the specifics, the moments, the emotions. I've done this 1000s of times. I regret every time I skip the strategy phase.

The interviewee won't be prepared or comfortable. I'll miss complete lines of questioning, an angle, or "digging" for certain stories.

The story might not even turn out to be a story.

That's why we don't even think about allowing our clients to skip any part of the planning process.

Do this correctly, and you'll have content that can easily yield a 20-100x ROI.

Deciding on shoot type

Before we start asking, we need to decide on the type of shoot when it comes to shooting video content. There are various options to consider. You can do an in-person shoot. This has several variations. One is sending out a videographer/ team to the subject. You can invite your client to a studio you rent. You can conduct an in-office shoot when your client comes in. You can coincide the shoot at an event where you know your clients will be. The other option is remote shooting.

Live Shoots

You can create amazing "in person" shoots with a filmmaker. This level of shooting adds a great deal to the design of the shoot. You can have amazing cinematic looks, capture great footage, and have a top notch look to your Video Case Story.

Live shoots have a few drawbacks overall. Something ALWAYS goes wrong with Video Production. That's why there's usually a looong list of credits in a film. Each person is an expert in just one of those elements, from scheduling, to wrangling, to set production, and, of course, light, sound, and cinematography.

Each person adds an additional human element, which means a possibility for the unknown. I've had some pretty embarrassing stories of hiring the wrong people for on-set work. I did a shoot where one crew member kept doing really stupid things during the shoot. My client, a big name in their industry, justifiably became angry and walked off set.

If you want a great Video Case Story, you'll want a great filmmaker AND someone who is a great interviewer. We'll talk about the interview part in a few. You can hope to find someone that is both. It's rare. The evening news sends out the journalist/camera person duo. Filmmaking has become easier in the digital age, but it still involves knowledge of logistics, set design, directing, camera work, lighting, and sound. Interviewing, especially for Video Case Stories, is a completely separate skill set.

You can go "cheap" with simply an iPhone and an interviewer from your office. This is good if you are collecting a lot of case stories and can circle back to the subjects. I've very rarely seen these turn out great.

Remember: The Video Shoot About Customer Experience is Still a Customer Experience

The shoot atmosphere is critical in a case story interview. People get nervous. You want to make your clients feel at ease. Make sure the entire team knows how to make them feel comfortable. You want smiling faces. You direct the client without ordering them. You want the team to be cognizant of the story material. You want them dressed appropriately.

In a B2B environment, you want the team to act a little extra professional.

And this is all BEFORE the interview, which is another, well, story.

There's also the "what if" element.

What if the interviewee reschedules, cancels, or ghosts you? This happens about 25% of the time. You're still paying for the video team.

What if your interviewee has stage/camera fright? This is a real thing. It happens even more if you don't have a great interviewee.

What if the story sucks? You're still paying for the video team, the space, and the scheduling.

Once you decide on an in person shoot, there's then the timing and location.

In Person Shoot at Your Location

One choice is to conduct the shoot in person at your location, which still requires an interviewer and a videographer.

It can be stressful finding the right videographer, finding the great interviewer, finding the time, and scheduling. You also want the right place in your location. You need to be able to set up all that equipment with multiple people in one space, have it quiet, have it confidential, have it personal, and have the right look to set up a decent video shoot.

Since you are investing, you'll want a good backdrop, which requires a great eye.

Pros: It's your location. You can also shoot "B-Roll" in your location, adding authenticity.

Cons: Most locations are not perfect for video shoots. You'll also have to interrupt other's work. If you work in a shared office building, often you will need permission from the office building.

Event Shoots

There's an event that brings all your clients together. It could be a conference, a tradeshow, or even your own client appreciation event.

The great part is you have all your people in one place. It's an effective way to capture a ton of interviews. I've done 25 interviews a day. That's a ton of content. Once again, you need to have a great videographer and a great interviewer, which are usually two different things.

You need to have the right location inside the event that is quiet enough. You'll want someone who's a wrangler to capture all the people that you want to interview and try to get them on a schedule. There's a lot that goes into this planning.

Pros: You can get everyone in one place and get a lot done in one day. It reduces production costs. These locations are often easier to load and unload equipment.

Cons: Your key interviewees might not show up. Interviewees will want to get back to the event. It's tough to create the right shoot environment from noise to backdrop. You'll still need other B-Roll options. Also, some event spaces are very strict about teams and cameras.

Studio Shoots

You can rent a studio and invite one client or several clients. Some studios have a Video team, and for some, you will bring your own. Obviously, there's an additional cost for the space. But it's the most controlled environment and the best chance for everything to work correctly.

Studio shoots require less setup time. There are various great backdrops. You have sound control.

We developed our own small studio, Garlic Studios, for this reason. We shoot more than Video Case Stories there. You can have a whole shoot day and knock out six months to a year of content. We also shoot podcasts, YouTube shows, online courses, and livestreams there. We have the full shoot suite available.

If you are serious about video for your business, it's smart to find one of these.

Client's Location

Going to a client makes it easier for them. You shoot them in their environment. This makes for awesome B-roll.

Client location shoots become a host of unknowns after that.

You never know the state of the location until you get there. People become strange when others enter their house or office. 90% of the time, office shoots are a surprise to everyone else in the office. I've had encounters with pets (both in office shoots and home shoots). I've had encounters with strange relatives who want to be film producers. You can arrive with a video team, and the client is not there.

Remote Shoots

We love remote video shooting. Zoom is now so easy, and there are many other applications coming out. People are used to online interviews.

Doing remote video shoots gets the video done faster.

It's easier for someone to say Yes. We suggest a remote shoot first, even if you want to do a live shoot. First, you never know if that story's going to go away.

Second, it prepares your client, the subject, to tell their story.

Third, remote shoots through Zoom often lead to a more intimate and candid interview experience. You don't have all the lights, the video camera, the additional people.

Zoom feels more like a confessional than an interrogation. The interviewees give more information, talk more, and are more willing to spend a longer time with you.

I suggest starting the remote shoot ahead of time for the reasons above. It's also easy to say you'll do both. You can call it a pre-shoot. You can call it a pre-interview so they know what to expect when they're at the live shoot.

Ultimately, the choice of type of shoot will depend on various factors, not just budget scheduling and the desired outcome. Where are you going to use these videos? How are you going to use them? That's why the goals and the planning come into place, regardless of the option chosen.

You want to make sure to have a strong interviewer and a great videography team set up to make sure it is a successful case story shoot.

Asking For the Video Case Story

Collecting great case stories can be a full-time job. You have to identify the stories and know when to ask and how to ask. It's a commitment that will pay off when you find those jackpot stories.

When to ask for the Case Story

Start with asking as soon as they get their result. Your client's business grew. They have a new smile. They sold the business. The divorce is final. They lost the weight. *Hopefully, this is not all one person.*

Ask as many people as possible. You never know who will say yes, who will be great, and who will just ghost you.

Make it a habit to ask for Video Case Stories throughout your entire customer lifecycle. Better yet, create systems and triggers to automatically ask for the story in your entire process.

You should create stories for your entire process, from your initial meeting and throughout the conclusion and even years beyond. This helps you to sell the entire process, not just the results. Demonstrating a great process speeds up sales. Selling the process makes your prospects and soon clients more comfortable.

You'll also want to ask well after the conclusion. This helps you to find the transformation. You want to document how the story evolved.

How to Ask

If you want to capture a compelling story about working with your company, it's crucial to ask the right way. One of the biggest mistakes you make is asking for testimonials. Why? Testimonials, as we've mentioned, make people think they're going to talk about you, and they put the focus on you rather than their story.

Asking for a testimonial makes people nervous. People want to do great for you. People think about what they're going to talk about. They want to have something prepared. Instead, ask for their story. When you reach out to a potential interviewee, avoid using that word "testimonial."

Ask for their story.

Now you shift the focus to their unique experience. People are natural storytellers. Rather than making it an endorsement of your company, you'll lead to a more authentic video and make it easier for them.

How much preparation will depend on how much you want to prepare the client. That is something that will depend on the strategy you are going for. By emphasizing the impersonal experience of the interviewee, you capture an engaging and authentic story. Remember, our goal is not just to promote your company.

We want to create stories that showcase the impact your company had on real people. In this way, you can create a powerful case story that resonates with your audience instead of a testimonial. That does all the things that we want it to. And we'll be able to find all those positioning patterns, those hooks that support the angles, as well as make additional discoveries.

Scheduling the Interview

So next up, we need to schedule the interview. Once we've asked how to schedule the case story interview to ensure that scheduling is done efficiently, I recommend you have a dedicated scheduler with a system. We found that it often takes asking four or five times, plus four or five follow-ups, to get this scheduled.

Obviously, if you have a set event or shoot day, the system changes.

It's not that people don't want to; it's that we're all busy. Scheduling is a time-consuming process, but it makes the case stories happen. It requires multiple follow-ups, including emails, calls, and text messages.

Once the interview is scheduled, it is important to send over all the necessary information, informing them how much you want to prepare them.

We want to talk about the interview format, the duration, and the location. Ensure the interviewee — if done remotely — has all the desired equipment for the remote interview. If you're going to do a live shoot, you'll want to tell them where and when, what to wear, what to expect, and how long it will take to make sure the experience is seamless. Have a follow-up plan in every place at every stage of the process when asking for the interview.

You provide an excellent experience for your clients, which improves the relationship.

Interviewees are much more comfortable, so you have a better shoot. Your client is likely to agree to do another story down the road.

They may even refer others to you because now they're even more invested in your business.

How many Video Case Story Interviews are the right number?

I get asked this question often. This answer is simple. As many as possible. You should aim to have a steady stream of case stories coming in from your clients and customers. I would suggest starting with at least two and actively collecting along the way.

This will help you to build up that whole tackle box of Video Case Stories. Collecting many and often will help you to keep a pulse on the market and a pulse on your clients. Find new opportunities, new positioning, and new hooks and angles as your business evolves.

Even if you think someone might not be good on video, ask them for their story.

They can remain anonymous. They don't even have to be on video. You can collect their voice and use photos. You never know who might surprise you. I've seen this so many times. The reverse can happen where you think someone's going to be great, and they're just okay or downright bad.

Now that we've set up the interviews, we are going to craft the questions and prepare for the interview process.

Scan here for bonus videos on this chapter.

https://linke.to/oKbE

13.1. CRAFTING THE QUESTIONS

"Do you have a list of questions?" Probably the most asked question of me is, "What camera should I use?"

You should have a list of questions, but they should be custom questions, and you should be asking, "How do I conduct a great interview?" instead of asking, "What questions should I use?" In the next chapter, we'll talk about conducting the interview, but let's talk about creating the questions.

The questions should follow the story. Connection, conflict, and conclusion. You also want questions that lead to the important details we discussed: Hooks, Angles, Specific Moments, Conclusions, and Transformations.

For example, if you are targeting moms in the connection section, you want to ask more about her life as a mom: "What's it like to be a mom?" Is she a working mom? Does she spend all her time with her kids? How many kids does she have? Dig deep into that.

In the B2B space, we want to understand the level of the person in business and a little about their history. We want to know about their role. Are they the owners? How long?

When you ask questions about the conflict, you want to know the evolution of the problem. You want to know when they first had a problem, what they tried to do about it, and their previous solutions. You want to devise those questions to pull out the entire story of the problem if there is one. In some cases, like a car accident, there might not be, per se, an evolution of the problem. There could be questions about never expecting the problem.

"Did you ever think you would have this problem?" is a great one. It will connect with future problems.

"Did you ever consider this was going to be a problem?"

We'll create questions to dig deeper.

Digging deeper into the conflict makes for a great story. You can speak to people all along their journey.

The conflict can include trying other companies and providers. You don't want to slander your competition. You do want to draw out why you are better.

The more conflicts you find, the better stories you will have. Digging into additional problems will generate ideas for more video content down the road, which we'll talk about in the last few chapters of this book.

Next are the conclusion questions. The conclusion questions would include things such as "What was the process like up until that first big win? What was the first big win? How did it feel? What other successes did you have along the way?" These are all questions that you want to know the answer to.

Most people go straight into this, and that's when it becomes a testimonial. But simply saying, "This attorney won me $1 million" or "I'm ranking on the first page of Google" doesn't really paint the picture of the conclusion. You want to talk a bit about that process. You want to find out about what it looked like when the client got those results.

And most importantly, in the conclusion, you want to ask about the transformation. What did that conclusion mean to you? What did it mean to you to get the $1 million settlement? What did it mean to you when your website was number one on Google? What does it mean to you now that your back pain is gone? How did your life immediately transform, and how did it transform in the long run?

You'll also want to prime questions that lead us to be able to interview them down the road. You can ask at the end of that, "Would you mind if we followed up with you? In six months to a year, you can see how life has changed and improved."

Obviously, this opens up your client to another part of the case story. This sets up a longer, more informative, more transformative story.

You will seed into your client's head looking for success down the road because it is easy for us to forget what someone did for us. It is easy for us to go back to our old way of thinking. Humans easily forget their struggles, and often the people that helped us.

On top of the story questions, we do want to dig into the questions of the issues that they have. You want to find their doubts.

What were their excuses along the way?

Were there any points where they thought this wasn't going to work?

These questions add more depth to the story. They also help you address these issues with prospective clients. Adding the problems adds authenticity to the story. Authenticity immerses the viewer in the story.

To recap: you want questions about

- Connection
- Conflict
- Conclusion
- Process
- Transformation
- Excuses and alibis

The two most powerful Story Questions

Once you have all of these questions formatted, you want to get into the two most powerful questions. Specificity in emotions in our stories and specificity in stories and descriptions bring the stories to life.

The first digging question is more of a command, "Describe when that happened."

That brings us into the story and brings us into the moment. As we discussed, people decide because of the moment. When you bring your viewer into the moment, they decide with their emotions. Emotions drive decisions. We all know this as marketers and salespeople. People decide because of emotions, and we want to make them feel emotions.

How powerful are emotions? Paul Zak research reveals studies of people watching a video. Videos full of emotion led the viewer to have empathy for the person in the video. When the viewer had empathy, they were roughly 30% more likely to make a positive decision at the end of the video, no matter what that decision was. In the example, they were asked to donate to an unrelated charity. There was a 30% increase in donations.

That's why testimonials will not work. Video Case Stories will work because they have emotions in them. So we want to get the emotions out.

After you have them describe what happened, you ask, "How did that make you feel?"

Very often, if you ask the right way, the interviewee will start to cry at this moment. I've had this actually happen more in B2B interviews than in "personal" interviews.

It just happened to me the other day on a podcast on True Law Stories, our podcast about lawyer stories. A lawyer was sharing her story about why she became an attorney, and I asked her to describe those moments and how she felt. She started to cry, and then I started to cry.

Eureka: We have a great story!!

Specificity and emotions are the gold in your stories. They are going to take your stories from good to great. Practice those two questions but yield them responsibly.

That level of emotion and empathy makes your stories memorable and makes the Big Fish take action.

Now you know how to create the questions. Understand that even if you have the best list of questions in the world, if you don't have a great interviewer on the other side, it's not going to work.

The interviewer is the key because you can't just send these questions to someone and expect a great story, moments, and emotions. We need someone to react to. We need someone to listen to. We need someone on the other side who cares about us.

Scan here for bonus videos on this chapter.

https://linke.to/RB69Rt

13.2 THE INTERVIEW

I am not an interviewer. I have conversations.
~ Werner Herzog

I remember when I first moved to New York City and I first encountered Charlie Rose. You may know him from some controversy on daily news shows, but he had his own show. And while some of his political views may have been controversial, his talent at interviewing was unparalleled.

He just had a way of asking questions that brought out the why behind the story. I watched and was intrigued not only by the interview itself but by the interview process. It was subtle, it was amazing, and the result was an interview that you saw nowhere else. So many TV interviews with stars on other shows just ask the same questions over and over and over again.

Charlie knew how to dig deep to find the emotions and real moments. That created an amazing show that just needed two chairs, a table, and a black backdrop. The show was simple and amazing. That's when I realized the power of great interviewing. It's something I've worked on and also worked with my team over the past 15 years.

Interviewing is a skill that is often undervalued. It's just such a critical part of collecting a great story. It is where you find the story and get it out to the world. If you're not an interviewer, you can miss out on seeing how great the story can be. The great journalists of our time ask questions that lead to a great story.

I believe that interviewing is one of the most important parts of the story. Those emotions that we talked about earlier must be found. Details almost never come out with just software, sending a list of questions, or simply sending a videographer out and pointing a camera at the person.

You have to look and dig for the stories. Great storytellers and great interviewers have a human connection with their subject. You need people who are interested to talk to them. The interviewee should care about the story and the person behind it. That's really where the beauty comes out.

You also want to review the strategy. You want to steer toward the angles and pull out the hooks.

You must know the major points you want to cover. You can't just run down a list of questions. Everything we've done up until now has set us up for this moment. A great interviewer guides the interviewee, asks probing questions, and gets specific details.

The interviewer needs to know how to ask questions. You need to care and ask questions like you care. They need to care about your client and have empathy. They need to care about your business and know where you're going with this. The interviewer also needs to know how to dig deep and how to work with that client in a conversational tone.

The interviewer needs to find those emotions, to find those moments, to find that specificity without upsetting the interviewee. The interviewer also needs to know when to be quiet. We just did an interview yesterday where a few questions led to a 55-minute story. Fifty-five minutes of your client talking about their story. That is content for years, and it is great content. You can use it in all the places that we've talked about to improve your sales and marketing. It is going to inform us in the next stages.

It is the great interview process that leads to people talking like this, opening up, and having those emotions, and that's why you must have a great interviewer if you're going to do this in-house. I suggest having someone besides yourself do the interview. I think it's just so weird when I ask people about me. It's just awkward. It's like going out on a date and after the date saying, "Hey, how did I do?" By the way, if you're doing that, you probably need to read a different book than this. I also think that if you're going to do this in-house, you should have someone who's already a good interviewer.

If you don't have that person, train them up. You may have a great account manager. That could be a good person. You might have a great paralegal. That could be a great person. Obviously, if you're an attorney, you can have other attorneys who are great at interviewing. Look for someone who's empathetic, understands the strategy, is good with people, is a conversationalist, and is not afraid to dig deep.

There are many great interviewers out there that you may be able to hire to do this, but do remember most videographers, most filmmakers are not these interviewers unless they are journalists or documentary makers.

One final bonus question, since you've read this far, the one question I learned to ask at the end of every interview, and it's a little awkward, but it often leads to amazing results: Is there anything we missed?

Sometimes people have a story that you haven't asked them about, and they're ready to talk about it. It's something additional that's there. I would say seven out of ten times, people just say, "No, that's everything. You did a great job." And one of my favorite compliments after an interview is, "That was really easy."

All that is because of strategy, because of caring, because of empathy. You now must sift and polish all that gold.

Scan here for bonus videos on this chapter.

https://linke.to/cBEzn

14.0 THE CSI PROCESS: CASE STORY INVESTIGATION

People leave us clues, Nick. They speak to us in thousands of different ways. It's our job to make sure we've tried to hear every single thing they've said.
~ Gil Grissom, CSI Vegas

Every interview has many different stories, hooks, and angles. There are keywords and different positioning opportunities. You will find opportunities for different versions. In most stories, you will find opportunities across sales, marketing, and operations.

Now you begin the Case Story Investigation Process (CSI) to uncover these opportunities. We will go through the following:

- Prospect Temperature
- Hooks and Angles
- Keywords
- Aha Moments
- Video Versions
- Distribution Strategy
- Additional Strategies

Prospect Temperature, Hooks, and Angles

First, you want to know what part of the journey you are focusing on. To simplify this, we'll use Cold, Warm, and Hot analogies.

Here's a quick overview of these terms. A cold visitor is "problem aware." They know they have a problem. They know they were in an accident. They know their marketing is not quite as good as it needs to be. They know their pants are getting tight. These are the toughest fish to land. They might be in the investigative phase, or they might just ignore the problem. It will take more to grab, hold their attention, and get them to take action.

A warm person in the journey is "solution aware." They know they need to find someone who is going to help them lose the weight. They know that they need to find an attorney. For the car accident, they know that they probably need someone to help them. The business owner needs help to drive more leads to improve their website.

A hot prospect knows about your business. They are "provider aware." They're comparing your business to other businesses. They're comparing it to doing it themselves. They're comparing it to not taking action.

These are the three main zones. I'll dive deeper when I talk about a system I call the storyboard blueprint. You dive into scenes. I used to do the Storyboard Blueprint first. The Case Story Tackle box will actually inform larger video strategies.

You're going to want to use different versions in different parts of your marketing. Awareness campaigns to people who don't know you use cold versions. These would be things like Facebook ads to demographics.

Provider-specific campaigns for people who are looking for a provider use warm versions. These would be Pay Per Click and SEO campaigns for your industry.

Hot versions are used when people are really thinking about working with you. Hot versions are used in The Fish in The Barrel strategy. These are great for follow up, retargeting, and conversion centric parts of your website.

Here's the evolution of hooks and angles in some different industries.

Divorce Attorney:

Cold: Hook: My husband was acting suspicious. ANGLE: Suspect your spouse is up to no good.

Warm: Hook: I really wanted an attorney who understood entrepreneurs. Angle: Business owner focused.

Hot: Hook: I was so nervous and unsure, but they were just a text away. Angle: Great Customer Service.

It makes your clients happier. I can't tell you how many times over the years I've used stories of my other clients. When a client isn't getting the results that they want, it will increase not only their results but also the chance of them staying with you. It'll increase their happiness. And as I mentioned, that leads to more referrals, more profits, and a better business.

You've spent the time on strategy. You've spent the time developing the questions. You have spent the time and money on getting a great interview. Now you have these amazing hooks and angles.

We will make great videos, but these hooks can be used elsewhere. These hooks make amazing social posts. You should use them in articles and blog posts. You'll also find they are email subject lines. Sometimes you find a quote that's just perfect for a headline for your website.

Uncover Keywords that Land the Biggest Fish the Fastest

Next up, you want to sift for keywords. I spent weeks on an SEO strategy for one contractor company. They were in a unique position. They had a bit of unique service. We then went into the Video Case Story collection process.

We had a shoot day. I interviewed six of their clients. Every single one of them mentioned a term we had not discussed before. It did not show up on any keyword searches.

That keyword was extremely valuable because his ideal clients all talked about it. There are so many of these keyword phrases that are ultra specific. They don't show up in keyword reports because they are low volume.

Big Fish are very specific in their searches. You want to be there because they are really ready to bite.

Now you can have one of your clients telling an amazing story when that keyword pops up and land that Big Fish. Ranking for highly specific, high intent keywords gets you in front of hot prospects at the perfect time. It's faster to rank videos, and as we discussed, great stories rank higher in all search engines.

A-Ha Moments

Interviewing clients leads to aha moments like keywords. It also leads to other opportunities. You'll find massive differentiators. You'll uncover new ways to serve them with current products and services, as well as new ones.

Video Versions

On average, we find 10 to 15 different versions of these videos, and you might think that's overkill. You never know what hook is going to grab someone. You never know how long someone will watch. And also, you want to design these for different platforms. The essential types of videos right now are micro content videos, sub-30-seconds up to 60-seconds.

Then you'll do 2-4 minute videos, 5-7 minute videos, and then the long form, ranging from 12 to 30 minutes for the case stories. If you've got an amazing case story with a lot of information, emotions, hooks, angles, and a great story arc, you can extend it to 30 minutes.

You might think your prospects will not watch 30 minutes. If it's entertaining, they will. You do it every night watching TV. We watch a lot of TV, especially reality TV, which is just a story. We'll watch for 30 minutes if it solves our biggest problems too. A lot of your prospects are in desperate need. They'll watch the 30 minutes.

Besides different lengths, you'll want to have different formats of the videos. It can be square, portrait 16 X 9, or landscape. It will depend on the platform. That's another reason we identified your platforms during the tacklebox. Gone are the days of simply making one video and posting it everywhere and being effective.

You can find the best lengths and dimensions by platform in www.Testimonialbook.com/toolkit.com

Platforms and Prioritize

You've already decided on platforms and campaigns in your Tackle Box.

Next prioritize those videos and decide which types of videos are best for those platforms. Depending on the campaign, decide if it's a cold, warm, or hot version. You'll decide the hook and the angle for that video. Make a whole list of these types of videos that we can create.

Let's say you create a YouTube campaign to convert more of your "Fish in The Barrel." If it's a good enough story, you could go for 5-7 minutes. YouTube is a 16x9 format for the main videos. Since you want to speak to current prospects, we would go with Warm to Hot Angles/Hooks.

Use the Interview in Other Videos

There are other videos you'll want to weave your case stories into, such as About Us, Process videos, how-tos, and FAQs. Start by concentrating on the case stories. Make a list of all the different types of videos from, micro-content to short form to long form videos. Then we will prioritize it based on our goals.

This is why I've stressed strategy so much. If you've skipped over that part, you're not going to know where to start. And even if you just get started, you're not going to use the videos properly. And then you're going to say, "Hey, Ian, this doesn't work."

Then you'll hate me, give me a bad review, and I'll cry myself to sleep.

So, please, to prevent my son from seeing me cry myself to sleep, START WITH STRATEGY.

The CSI case story investigation allows us to dig deep, find all the opportunities, find the types of videos we should create, and then prioritize them. Now you move into post-production.

Scan here for bonus videos on this chapter.

https://linke.to/v2Bv

15.0 POST-PRODUCTION

Now that we have our list of prioritized videos, we move into post-production for each of these videos. These videos are going to be used for years.

Investing time and effort in finding the right skill sets in post-production increases the effectiveness and longevity of these videos exponentially.

Great post-production can mean the difference between a few views and thousands of views. Post-production can also mean the difference between the video working at all and you using it for five plus years like many of our clients do. Some of our clients have even used these videos for ten plus years, and they're still working.

Just last year, we had a dental client that landed a Big Fish, a five-figure case from a case story we did over six years ago. That's direct value. That's not accounting for all the people who saw it who came in and said nothing about it. So post-production, like all our other processes, is here for a reason. It is a system we've developed over the years to improve your videos and to make them absolutely amazing. Follow this system, and you'll magnify the effectiveness of every video.

Temperature, Topic, Platform

First, you start with temperature and topic. You want to know where the viewer is in their journey. Then you need to know the platform because this will dictate the format, the length, and the style of the video. Luckily, you did all of that in the CSI review.

So everything we did prior to this improves the chances of being able to use the story in many different ways. Someone's ready to work with you and about to spend money and time with you and wants to absorb more stories. They want to absorb more content. They want to reaffirm their decision to move forward. They are a "Hot" prospect.

Hot prospects are almost ready to work with you. This video will go on YouTube and be on the website. The case story can be up to five minutes long. It could be a little longer, but we don't want it too short. Do not use a lot of text overlays in YouTube videos. People watch YouTube videos more often with sound. You do generally have a larger screen and can do more imagery and things with the footage.

That means they'll spend more time watching the videos. And since this is a hot version, talk much more about your specific value propositions and angles. For your business, use those hot angles. Those angles might be customer service, your experience, or even your accolades.

The Video Elements

Next you will put together the elements of the story; the essential elements will be the hook, the angle, and then the connection, conflict, and conclusion.

Now, the specific format of each video will sometimes shift how these are woven together. But if you're really dialed into your ideal client, which you should be, a great hook will grab their attention. Connection hooks are great here.

"Oh, this person is just like me."

You want to call out specific people you want to work with. You also want to send away the people you don't want to work with.

Conflict hooks generally work for all temperatures. "I never thought this would happen to me."

Conclusion hooks can also work for all temperatures, especially if the conclusion calls out a specific result. Use your business name in hot hooks. Don't use it in cold.

"I closed a 7-figure deal from YouTube." Cold conclusion hook examples.

"Ian's YouTube Strategy attracted a 7-figure deal in the first six months." Hot conclusion hook

There also could be a big mystery hook. Curiosity is one of the most powerful tools in content creation and copywriting. I alluded to it in:

"I never thought this would happen to me."

"I opened our leads list and couldn't believe it."

These types of hooks come out of great questions and great interviewing.

These are elements of great direct response copywriting.

Everyone on our team has at least 30 hours of training in direct response copywriting. This skill is critical to EVERY marketer. I really think every business owner should know it.

I've worked with my friend and client Jeremy Weisz to create the Giants of Direct Response. It's over 100 classes on direct response copywriting. It's available in the toolkit at www.Testimonialbook.com/toolkit.com.

Review the Content

Whoever's working on it is probably too close to it. So first, have someone review it for strategy. You want to make sure that it is in line with your strategy. Next have someone review it for story continuity and story elements to make sure it makes sense. Once that is done, have someone proof it for any little errors.

Add Visual Elements

Now the content is dialed in. It's time to add on elements. Imagery engages the entire brain with graphics, imagery, and sound effects. You might have identified important statistics. You should have identified visuals in the strategy portion. B-roll footage tells the stories that will be layered on.

The more we engage the brain, the more someone is into the story, the more they're likely to remember the story, and the more they're likely to take action. Visual effects B-roll, which is additional footage layered on top of it, and supporting graphics all play a role.

You can show more leads coming through in a graph, but you can also use emotional equivalence. A beach symbolizing serenity, holding a child's hand to give the feeling of family, or a blue bear in a suit to give a PowerPoint and to represent — yeah, I did just say a blue bear in a suit. A pattern interrupt is a powerful tool that we need to use at times in imagery.

The mention of a blue fuzzy bear in a suit was not expected, and it snapped back your attention. Pattern interrupts should also be used to "stop the scroll." You are battling for attention. This is one thing that you should work on continuously. You are battling for attention. Don't be afraid to be outlandish here.

No one's going to watch your case stories if they look like everything else on the feed. That click is highly unlikely. You want to use imagery and clips to stop the scroll and get the click.

Once you get them, you want to add engagement. Another way to do this is dynamic text. 80% of Social Media videos are viewed without sound. Great text that moves, shakes, and spins (Dynamic Text) adds to engagement and message reinforcement.

Quality Assurance

Now, once we've added text overlays and all these elements, we want to make sure it works. So, we want to move into quality assurance. Have you ever watched the credits at the end of a Marvel movie? Most likely, yes, because they do such an awesome job in the post-credit scenes.

There are a lot of people working on those movies. There are people with all sorts of skill sets. Many of those people are just there for quality assurance.

When my wife and co-founder of our company, Jessica Garlic, worked in animation for places like Nickelodeon, Miramax, and Disney, she always had a specific responsibility. For a while, it was just the animation of special effects. I say "just," but that was an important job. Special effects are very important in cartoons.

Now, could one person do all the animation? Sure. It would take a lot longer, and people are great at every single part of this. A good story editor is not necessarily the best strategist. They're definitely not the best at sound effects. They may not be the best visual editor.

Each one of these is a very specific skill set. On top of it, there would be no quality assurance because you get too close to what you're doing. It's easy to make mistakes and miss those mistakes.

If you can't afford or don't know a team, find a partner to help you out. Give another business owner this book, and work on it together.

You can also fill out the application at VideoCaseStory.com/GetStarted. We'll help you to find the right partners, strategists, videographers, and editors.

Now you understand the importance of making this great. You should look to have a team work on your Video Case Stories.

There are different types of team members.

You have story people. You have distribution people. You have quality assurance. Just like in a film, you have a director or producer and a project manager. I'm going to beat this horse to death. Your case stories are a critical part of your business. So, if you have the resources, look to find people who are experts in their craft.

The Four Questions for Video Success

I ask four questions of everyone working on the video in our company. You should always ask these questions of the video editor and anyone else working on your video. If it's just you working on it, you should ask these four questions over and over and over again.

Question #1: Who are we talking to? You've decided that already. You have to remember it. That's why you've done all that strategy.

Question #2: Where are they in their journey? I want you to know as specifically as possible. I want you to be able to tell their story. What's going on in their life, their business? Where are they physically? What platform are they on? What are their burning problems? These all should have been addressed in the Case Story Interview.

Question #3: Why would they pay attention to this?

What's going to grab their attention? How are we stopping the scroll? Where are pattern interrupts? What are those hooks? Why would they keep paying attention to it? How are we going to keep their attention? Are there any lulls in this? This is critical to making a video that keeps attention. We've gone over this a lot. Attention is everything in marketing.

Question #4: What do we want them to do next? Now, everyone says, "I want them to call us and make an appointment." Every video should not be driving a phone call. Those should generally only be "Hot" versions.

Every video has a different purpose. One purpose is to watch another video. Another is subscribing to your channel. Other purposes are signing up for a course, downloading a lead magnet or event going to your website, watching another video, watching a series of videos, or just commenting and sharing. You don't want to have too many calls to action. I would suggest two, maximum.

The better you answer these questions, the better the chance of success. They are simple questions, but they are not always easy to answer.

"Version done is better than Version None." – My T-Shirt

No video is going to be perfect. Get these videos out in a timely fashion. Use this process, trust the process, and realize this.

The good video (Version done) out there beats the perfect video not completed (Version None) EVERY SINGLE TIME.

Now it's time to really get those videos out there.

Scan here for bonus videos on this chapter.

https://linke.to/k83T

16.0 DISTRIBUTION STRATEGY

Such a weird thing. These videos won't yield results unless you consistently employ them.

Start with the low hanging "Fish."

Start with your Fish in the Barrel. If you haven't done so already, make sure to download the Fish in the Barrel strategy from the resource page www.Testimonialbook.com/toolkit.com You have prospects you are not closing because you are not showing them the value of working with you.

Your new Video Case Stories will quickly fix that.

The Fish in the Barrel strategy uses both warm and hot versions of the stories repeatedly. These are all of the places people can encounter you, including cold leads, dead leads, referrals, and even referrers.

Make cold leads, warm leads, then hot.

Cold leads hit your presence for whatever reason. It could be a blog. It could be a search query or a shared post. If they are interested, they may peruse and then forget. They become fish in your barrel. Having multiple Video Case Stories and versions keeps them engaged.

You should never stop marketing to dead leads. I can't tell you how many clients I've closed in the years after first encountering them. You never know which story is going to resonate.

Referrals are not slam dunks anymore. They will research you and end up on another's presence. Keep your stories in front of them — the more stories, the more times they will engage you.

Ask for Referrals without Asking

Asking people for referrals is tough. It's much easier to say, "Here's our latest story." The story triggers the referral. It could be the connection. "I know someone just like that." The conflict usually triggers the issue. "That problem sounds familiar." The conclusion is very shareable, especially when it's transformative and will get engagement. "I want that result, or I know someone that does." By doing this alone, you can easily achieve a 10X return on investment within the first two years.

Sales and marketing go hand in hand, except much of the time, they don't. You should arm your sales force with these powerful stories immediately. Fish in the Barrel leads to this. Send case stories before any prospects meeting. Different versions allow you to present different stories. Taylor McMaster's team at the Virtual Training and Staffing Company transformed their sales process with this simple act. You can see her video when you sign up for the ToolKit. Next, have your sales team install a system cross-referencing case stories with lost leads. I had a staffing company ghost us, and now they are getting Taylor's Case Story. Your sales team (even if it's just you) should feature these in their email signatures.

PRO TIP: Pare down your signature to a SINGLE link. Two links if you want "Click to call." This also adds a reason to drive prospects to your YouTube channel.

Next, have your sales team develop the habit of adding them to the proposals. That's a 32% increase in sales. Now you are ready to amplify the rest of your marketing. Start with your Video Case Stories. Make it a habit to incorporate Video Case Stories into every marketing effort. Consider your client's journey and identify the platforms they frequent.

Review the Video Case Story subject. Ask them what platforms they are on. Then create content around that, STARTING with the case story. "Are you trying to do this? Here's someone who had the same problem. Here are three things you can do right now." I developed the Storyboard B blueprint for that reason. Each prospect is on a journey. You need to develop content for that journey. We'll dive deeper into that in the videos section.

Now, let's delve into cold ads. Cold traffic is enticing because it brings new leads and untapped potential that didn't come from referrals. However, these leads need to be warmed up. Use case stories as cold traffic ads, using hooks specific to the platform. Engage people who are unfamiliar with you by presenting a cold version of the story. For instance, use phrases like "I never thought I'd be in this situation" or "I never thought I'd overcome this challenge." Such stories resonate with audiences and create memorable impressions.

Let's discuss distribution, specifically cold outreach in sales. When making cold calls, use Video Case Stories to transform them into warm calls. Ask if they have a problem similar to what the story portrays and suggest they watch it. Even if they aren't ready to buy immediately, they will remember the story. This methodology is time-tested and proven. Additionally, apply these techniques to sales training and explore other marketing avenues.

Trade shows, for example, offer excellent opportunities. Play Video Case Stories in the background without sound to capture attention. This works especially well if you have a recognizable presence at the trade show. Then, of course, there's the red elephant riding the white gorilla in the video distribution room.

Scan here for bonus videos on this chapter.

https://linke.to/lOrA6N

16.1 DOMINATE WITH YOUTUBE: THE #1 HACK AND THE SIMPLE OPTIMIZATION FORMULA

YouTube is the #2 most used search engine. It's where we go to learn, to be entertained, to be distracted, and to discover.

YouTube is the only platform that's on our TV.

YouTube makes it easy to save videos, revisit and share them.

YouTube videos have worked for years. Every other platform's videos work for months.

For every minute a prospect spends on your website, they spend ten minutes on your YouTube channel.

From C-suite execs, to small business owners, to moms - all making decisions on YouTube.

No generation says, "YouTube isn't for me."

I started my first agency after Google purchased YouTube. I instantly saw what we were going to be able to do. We could now deliver the perfect story when someone looked for it.

Few believed me when I said every business needed to be there. We did websites and other services to convince people that they needed to be on YouTube.

Since then, YouTube moved to the center of our marketing efforts. While I hate to date this book, I'm betting the trend of YouTube dominance will only continue. YouTube has become the center space for learning and entertainment as use skyrockets. This makes the platform the best opportunity for you to create content and engage with potential, current, and past clients.

I urge you to consider your customers' entire journey. Dive deep into every scene in their life and create content to benefit them. Video Case Stories, created as prescribed, do the trick. You'll want to create other videos too. Optimize your videos on YouTube accordingly.

Every minute you spend on YouTube Strategy will yield years of results.

On top of all the other benefits, YouTube is one of the few platforms that you have both intention and attention to capture.

Most social media marketing aims to capture attention. Social media marketing aims to pull away the viewer from what they are doing. Your business social media must fight to wrestle attention from cats and puppies and babies.

Yes, on YouTube, you must often battle against those things as well. The mind-set of a YouTube user holds a huge differentiator. YouTube users are there with intention as well.

Intention means YouTube users want to accomplish something. People sit on TikTok, Facebook, and Instagram, aimlessly. We often visit YouTube with a purpose, an intent.

High intent means your prospects look to solve that problem, find someone to help them, or research the provider on YouTube. This difference in use means a difference in the mind of your prospect. Intention means viewers absorb quality content, answering the intent, not just flitter from short to short.

A few magical things happen.

The viewer informs the platform of their intent, so YouTube will now try additional relevant videos. Since Google ties to YouTube, that data passes back and forth.

Now they are in the mindset to discover and learn. The other magical piece occurs here. The viewer may get distracted. The intent of their previous video follows them around.

And they can save it for later. YouTube becomes a personal library, filled with distraction and education. We are fine being shown relevant education to our latest search, even when in distraction mode.

Despite what you think, It's not a straight journey.

Take my ukulele Journey. Not counting fourth grade recorder lessons, the ukulele was my first instrument. I've become tolerable over the years. My learning journey started ten years ago on YouTube.

Did I ONLY watch ukulele videos on YouTube? Of course not. I watch cat videos. I watch stand-up comedians. I learned how to live on a lake. I investigated what kind of boat was perfect for me (a pontoon). I also discovered that there's almost no chance of me ever doing any cool wakeboard tricks.

I come to YouTube with high intent, often for ukulele lessons. You can find my long list of ukulele lessons on my uke YouTube playlist. YouTube knows my INTENT and shows me uke lessons when I'm watching stand-up comedy or Star Wars breakdowns.

Those Playlists have lasted for years. I've spent money with the teachers on those playlists.

I also discover and learn the latest marketing techniques. I create playlists and watch these videos in increments. I've researched the latest in economics and financial markets.

I share all these videos often and with other professionals. What other platform do you readily share outside of the platform?

Your prospects and clients use YouTube the same way. They have intent, especially when you send them there to watch your AMAZING Video Case Stories. Your audience will then see your content when watching other things. You're grabbing attention that's based on intention.

You win even if your videos are not watched.

Google plus YouTube.

You also have the INTENTION of the biggest search engine, Google. YouTube videos show up in Google searches. Your audience uses Google many times a day to solve their problems and answer their questions. Your YouTube videos can show up there, especially when they are powerful stories.

I say audience because you have a chance to stay in front of everyone in your circles, especially current clients and customers.

Your Video Case Story and other videos should be there, LEADING to YouTube. Google's search passes to your YouTube video. Someone hits your YouTube channel with that intent. They encounter your stories and get to know you in a "safe space." Now YouTube will show your relevant videos to them when they are watching Star Wars, comedians, and ukulele videos.

And they won't feel interrupted because they had the intent.

YouTube Manages First, Second, and Tenth Impressions.

We've talked about your online reputation. I'm not just talking about reviews. You need to pay attention to what the searches look like for you and your business.

You dress well, at least now, from the waist up. You have a nice office. You spent months on that pretty website. You had way too many meetings about your logo (which I guarantee almost no one remembers).

Then you ignore what it looks like where your clients and prospects encounter you most: search.

Prospects, referrals, current customers, and potential dates continually research you. My young (8-15-year-old) family members all sheepishly tell me they watched all my YouTube videos.

YouTube allows you to not only control what your audience sees. You can take advantage of it. Optimizing Video case Stories for these searches should be your first priority. Every time someone searches for you for any reason, a customer tells an amazing story of transformation.

Optimizing for YouTube Intent

Optimize your Video Case Stories for a variety of keywords and searches. There are some obvious keywords. You'll have discovered some new ones in the CSI process.

Optimize Video Case Stories for:

- Your name
- Your business name
- Your business name + reviews
- Big problems you solved
- Unseen problems you've solved
- Specific services
- Specific outcomes

Aim to rank for your name or industry keywords related to the problems your audience faces. Your stories can rank for your service, i.e., Warm Stories.

Think of these as "Directory Keywords."

- Chiropractor Orlando
- Divorce Lawyer Chicago
- Digital Agency for Ecommerce Companies

Your stories come up instead of just your website. You can get your Videos to rank in Google for these.

Optimizing means capturing their INTENTION with keywords which we found during the CSI process. You'll want ATTENTION-grabbing headlines as well. Use hooks you pulled out during the CSI session to grab the attention.

SEO (Search Engine Optimization) has evolved massively and will continue to do so. Everyone looks for the hack. The good and bad news is hacks have become fewer and far between. Google has so much data on every user, and an AI algorithm continues to use that to improve search experience. Still, links are key to the authority of the content. The knowledge difference between Google search and YouTube search is YouTube has 100% knowledge of your content consumption.

YouTube knows almost everything about the YouTube users viewing the video. YouTube knows which video led them there. YouTube knows the search. YouTube knows the thumbnail and headline. YouTube knows where the videos were "rewatched," where they paused, and where the viewer dropped off YouTube. YouTube's algorithm can truly optimize all content.

I know that sounds complicated. It is. But there's a simple (but not easy) secret to ranking your videos.

The Super Simple Optimization Secret

The #1 key to great YouTube SEO (or optimizing for any platform) is knowing what the platform wants. Each platform will have certain goals, and the granular goals will change. YouTube will prioritize unique features and reward users.

Overall, YouTube wants one big thing: as much watch time as possible. The more people watch and the longer they stay on the platform, the more money YouTube makes in ads. You want to optimize for total watch time. It's simple. I didn't say it was easy.

Make Great Stories and Rank Higher

We want people with intent to watch stories that relate to their problem. Education content is great. Usually, educational content will not HOLD attention. We may want to learn how to make $1 million in three days, but will you really watch 45 minutes of step-by-step education? No, you'll watch a little and come back.

You will watch the story of someone like you and their journey to making $1 million (or losing it). That's why it's so important to make great stories. Your hooks grabbed the attention of the audience. Your stories keep them.

Your story may grab the attention on YouTube with that intent. Your prospects were looking for information on growing their business, then your story about "SaaS company overcomes Facebook ad dumpster fire to triple MRR in six months" grabs their attention.

Your viewer may have looked for "Best Ad Agency for SaaS companies."

"Florida Healthcare Entrepreneur prosecuted by Federal Government for seven years, Saved by Florida Federal Criminal Attorneys."

This will grab the attention of almost any entrepreneur.

"50-year-old man struggles with back pain entire life transformed Online Trainer into Fitness Model."

Almost every 50-year-old man struggles with back pain and wants to be a fitness model.

You grab their attention. In your amazing Video Case Story, your best customer now details their problems and the process of transformation with you.

You gain the ranking, the view time, and spend time with your best customers. The story might even be shared. You start to rank in Google.

YouTube rewards you by ranking the video higher and showing it to more customers.

The Simple YouTube Optimization Criteria

YouTube wants view time. YouTube measures total view time, so longer videos rank higher.

YouTube also wants a percentage of total view time. They want to know if your videos keep people's attention. We do that, of course, with great stories.

Use different keywords along your customer's journey. Create different versions of the video for different keywords on YouTube. This comes from a different story.

For Example, a fitness entrepreneur like ResetU would have:

Cold Keywords like "Am I overweight?"

Warm Keywords like "Best fitness programs for busy entrepreneurs" and "Best Personal Trainers for Injured Athletes."

Hot Keywords like "ResetU Results" and "Reset U Reviews"

Each of these places is an opportunity to have a Video Case Story ranking.

Each of these videos could come from a single interview.

Optimize Your YouTube Videos with These Four Questions

The four steps to great YouTube SEO are answering the four questions from the Post-Production chapter.

Let's review them one more time. They are that important.

Who are we talking to? You answer this through case story goals. You know who you want to attract and gain case stories that are like that person.

What do they want right now? You learn this through knowing a thing about the prospect's scene, the moment in their life. You generalize this by using cold, warm, or hot terminology. Your prospects are looking for answers to their problem, a specific solution, or someone to help them. You optimize for this by uncovering the keywords and hooks that will grab their attention at any point in the journey.

Remember, sometimes what they want right now is to just be entertained. Thus comes our next question.

Why should they pay attention to this (and continue to)? The hook grabs attention. The story arc holds attention.

You can teach all day. You can give away all your secrets. Nothing will hold attention better than a great story. The more time you spend crafting a great story, the more people will watch. The more people watch, the more YouTube will reward you. The more your perfect audience sees your video, the more they will see it at the perfect time.

Does this REALLY speak to your perfect audience at that moment? The better you answer that question, the better the video will do.

You laid the groundwork already by following the Video Case Story process.

The marketing success and the money all come with the last question.

What do we want them to do next? You can get all the views in the world. If it doesn't improve YOUR results, was it worth it?

Videos with millions of views litter YouTube, owned by broke creators. You must optimize for what you want them to do next.

Your major goal should be moving them down the path to the next point in their journey: working with you. This may be watching another video. This could be comments, likes, or subscribes. It could be downloading a course, joining your membership, or setting up a consultation.

In general, here are the CTAs (Calls to Action) by temperature.

Cold viewers, you want to watch another video, comment, or subscribe.

Warm viewers subscribe, email opt in, or make a discovery call.

Hot viewers set an appointment and buy more.

You should have a goal for the video. What do you want the video to do/viewer to do next? The other three questions, who, why, and where, support what you want the viewer to do next.

That's it. Concentrate on the journey, on feeding YouTube, and on aligning with your goals. You've now created great content.

YouTube Hacks

Now it's time to fill out your YouTube channel with different types of videos. Elevate from a Good Storyteller to a Great Storyteller.

Scan here for bonus videos on this chapter.

https://linke.to/Gfvquv

17.0 BECOMING A BETTER (VIDEO) STORYTELLER

When it comes to videos, becoming a storyteller goes beyond just Video Case Stories (GASP).

These videos include About Us/Bio Videos, Process Videos, and FAQs.

About Us and Bio Videos

About Us videos are the first ones to focus on. I say "ones" because you'll want different versions. You'll want a longer video, a shorter video, one for hiring and inspiring your team, and individual About Us videos, aka Bios. The About Us video is the second most used on your website after the homepage. This is the moment prospects want to like and trust you more. The simple key to great About Us videos is it's "About Them," your clients and prospects. What's the best way to do that? You guessed it.

By incorporating Video Case Stories into your About Us videos, you'll witness a remarkable difference. Case stories woven into it add depth and impact to your message, making it more engaging and meaningful.

Bio videos, similar to About Us videos, are often overlooked. Many businesses make the mistake of simply stating what they do in a 30 second video. But what really matters is what you do for your clients. Showcase stories of how your team has helped clients, highlighting their successes and how they have been empowered. These stories will make potential clients recognize the value and benefits of working with you. You'll also want case stories from other team members.

Process Videos

Process videos are another valuable tool. Process videos tear down objections and make it easier to say Yes, reduce fears, and "Futurecast" your prospect. Your viewers will see themselves in the process of working with you. You may want to create multiple process videos explaining how to work with you, how to reach your office, or what to expect in different scenarios. The more proprietary you can make your process, the better. These videos don't just provide value; they engage and educate viewers. By showcasing your unique processes, viewers can see themselves in the journey and start envisioning how they can benefit from working with you. Video Case Stories highlight the process and excite your prospects about the work.

How To/FAQs and Video Blogs

Other videos you should be making include:

- Video Frequently Asked Questions (FAQs)
- Video Blogs
- How To Videos

Webinars, in particular, are powerful tools for educating and engaging your audience. They fall under the umbrella of how-to videos, which should teach viewers how to accomplish tasks related to your industry. Ask any webinar expert, and they will tell you to start your webinar with Video Case Stories.

To determine which videos to create, consider using a storyboard blueprint. You'll have access to our document at www.Testimonialbook.com/toolkit.com. People decide because of the scene. You storyboard their journey and then walk through each scene. The Video Case Story and Tackle Box processes gave you great insight into their scenes.

The Storyboard Blueprint helps you understand your customers' journeys and identify the moments when they can benefit from your expertise. By aligning your videos with these moments and incorporating mimetic desire — showing how others have benefited — you create engaging and captivating content that speaks to the other decision-making factor: The Situation.

Your Video Case Stories will make all these videos great. You are now on the journey to being The Best Storyteller.

Scan here for bonus videos on this chapter.

https://linke.to/cNECr

18.0 THE BEST STORYTELLER WINS

We've shown you how to become a good storyteller. The work is now yours — to become The Best Storyteller. I mentioned some of the best.

Steve Jobs. Walt Disney. Look at legends like Thomas Edison, Ben Franklin, and even Jesus Christ. They were the best storytellers. Light bulbs, electricity, the USA, and the largest religion on the planet are all famous because of Great Storytelling. You can't argue with those results (even if it does sound like a beer commercial). The best storyteller wins.

Throughout my journey, I've come to realize that there's no business problem that can't be solved in some way, shape, or form by the Video Case Story solution. This system has the power to guide you in the right direction, spark innovation, and create that unstoppable flywheel effect in your business. It can inspire your team, boost your sales, and supercharge your marketing efforts. But only if you take action.

One of my annual reads is *The Greatest Salesman in the World* by Og Mandino. It's filled with scrolls for success. One scroll gets me going every time.

> *I will act now.*
>
> *Never has there been a map, however carefully executed to detail and scale, which carried its owner over even one inch of ground. Never has there been a parchment of law, however fair, which prevented one crime. Never has there been a scroll, even such as the one I hold, which earned so much as a penny or produced a single word of acclamation. Action, alone, is the tinder that ignites the map, the parchment, this scroll, my dreams, my plans, my goals, into a living force. Action is the food and drink that will nourish my success.*
>
> *I will act now.*

I've given you the map. I've seen people take different offshoots of it, but everyone who takes the action, the consistent action, wins.

As my dad, John Garlic, said, "Action begets action." Act now. Become the best Storyteller.

Go land those Big Fish.

Scan here for bonus videos on this chapter.

https://linke.to/SDR4Kg

P.S. I hope you were inspired, excited, and educated by this book. PLEASE help me to stay inspired and leave a review on Amazon. Just scan the QR code below!

Your feedback and your stories mean the world to me.

Thanks for taking me on your journey,

Ian Garlic

Made in the USA
Monee, IL
12 November 2026

c4856828-f42d-4678-8cc4-66d3491921d9R01